ISLAN

CA

WORLD RELIGIONS AND ECOLOGY

This series looks at how each of five world religions has treated ecology in the past, what the teaching of each has to say on the subject, and how that is applied today. Contributors from a variety of backgrounds in each religion put forward material for thought and discussion through poetry, stories, and pictures as well as ideas and theories.

The series is sponsored by the World Wide Fund for Nature, who believe that a true understanding of our relation to the natural world is the best step towards saving our planet.

Titles in the series are:

BUDDHISM AND ECOLOGY
Martine Batchelor
and Kerry Brown

CHRISTIANITY AND ECOLOGY
Elizabeth Breuilly
and Martin Palmer

HINDUISM AND ECOLOGY: Seeds of Truth
Ranchor Prime

ISLAM AND ECOLOGY
Fazlun M. Khalid
with Joanne O'Brien

JUDAISM AND ECOLOGY
Aubrey Rose

ISLAM
AND
ECOLOGY

Edited by

Fazlun M. Khalid

with

Joanne O'Brien

CASSELL

Cassell Publishers Limited
Villiers House, 41/47 Strand, London WC2N 5JE, England
387 Park Avenue South, New York, NY 10016–8810, USA

First published 1992

British Library Cataloguing-in-Publication Data
A catalogue record for this book is available from the British
Library.

Library of Congress Cataloging-in-Publication Data
Available from the Library of Congress.

ISBN 0–304–32377–2

Cover picture and illustrations at the beginning and end of
chapters by

Panda symbol © 1986 World Wide Fund for Nature

Typeset by Fakenham Photosetting Limited, Fakenham, Norfolk
Printed and bound in Great Britain by Mackays of Chatham plc,
Chatham, Kent

CONTENTS

Whenever the Prophet Muhammad is mentioned in the text, his name is followed by the letter 'S'. This is an abbreviated form of the phrase 'Peace be on Him' or 'May Allah bless Him and grant Him peace' which is said by Muslims in Arabic as a sign of respect.

The Qur'an is the holy book that contains the word of Allah revealed to the Prophet Muhammad (S). It is used throughout this book as a common source of reference by the contributors.

Also used are quotations from the Hadith (traditions). The Hadith are a record of the Sunna, that is, what the Prophet (S) did or said and are universally accepted by Muslims as an interpretation of the Qur'an itself. There are six major compilations of the Hadith and they are usually referred to by the scholar ('alim) who compiled them: Bukhari, Muslim, Ibn Majah, Abu Daud, Tirmidhi and Nasai. Their works are referred to by their names in this book. Holding a place above that of the Hadith compilers are the scholar-jurists (faqih, pl. fuqaha) who were responsible for creating the four schools of law (fiqh) in Sunni Islam. These schools of law, which have a lot in common with each other, are popularly known by the name of the scholar-jurist who originated them: Shafi, Hanafi, Hanbal and Malik. Any references to these works will be dealt with by quoting the scholar-jurist himself followed by his work, e.g. Imam Malik, *Muwatta*. There are also references in the book to other sources like *Mishkat al Masabih* and *Riyadh as Salihin*. These are compilations of

Hadith by scholars and jurists who came much later on but who nevertheless based their work on the earlier sources. They have a special place in Islamic scholarship and are often quoted by writers. In this book we go no further than referring to the name of the work, as many editions are in print and an excess of detail could distract the reader. There are also numerous references by the contributors to this book to other scholarly works. We merely refer to them by name in the text but where possible we attempt to give more detail in the references at chapter ends.

The Muslim calendar is dated from the time that the Prophet Muhammad (S) and his followers took refuge in Madina because of strong opposition to Islamic teachings in Makkah (Mecca). The journey to Madina is known as the Hijrah; each year in the Muslim calendar is followed by AH, the abbreviated form of 'After Hijrah'. The first year of the Muslim calendar corresponds to 622 of the Christian calendar. When the term CE appears after dates it refers to 'Common Era' and is used instead of AD.

An Arabic phrase is written at the beginning of each chapter. This is a phrase in praise of Allah which is said by Muslims before beginning any task. It is translated as:

'In the name of Allah, the Compassionate, the Merciful'.

PREFACE

It could be said that the essays that follow will throw some beams of light in the darkness that is about to descend on us. I have a mental picture of people sharing in a massive banquet completely oblivious to the fact that the roof is crumbling and will eventually come crashing down on their heads. There are other people standing at the exits warning the diners to leave but they don't take any notice since the meal is too good.

We are destroying and consuming our inheritance on which our survival depends and most of us do not even understand the real nature of the problem. We are not confronted with just another disaster; this will overshadow all past disasters put together. What is unfolding is a debacle of vast proportions but it will not come suddenly. Perhaps it is the stealth by which the disaster threatens to overtake us that makes us so complacent. What you see on your television screens and read in the newspapers about these matters is directly concerned with you the reader. They are not things that happen 'out there'. Make no mistake about it, the process of environmental change has begun. Nature is changing and the survival of the human race is at stake. We have to live with the knowledge that we caused this disaster as mindless and selfish consumers. We can be shamed by this as the process unfolds but there is no room for further complacency.

Scientists predict that it may be too late to turn the tide but what we can do at best is contain the apocalypse. This responsibility rests on our shoulders; it is not a problem for the other person, the other town or the other country. Each one of us must do what we can with as many people as possible, firstly to inform others and then to form action groups in our neighbourhood, schools, places of work, in fact anywhere and with anyone who is concerned. Islam provides the framework within which this can be done and our model is the Prophet Muhammad (S). We have to return to his example of the simple lifestyle or we may perish.

Many books have already been written on the issues we cover, but I believe this to be the first attempt at a comprehensive presentation of the Islamic position on ecology. It has been a privilege to work with the other contributors to this book. Although each deals with separate aspects of nature and the environment there are inevitable overlaps because within Islam everything is interrelated.

I am saved the task of making disclaimers because of the remarkable unanimity amongst the contributors. But as the editor I take responsibility for any factual errors that may occur in the text. Firstly, my thanks to the contributors. Yassin Dutton was born in Sussex, England, and obtained a master's degree in Arabic from Oxford University, where he is currently researching Islamic law; he was previously Imam of the Norwich mosque. Mawil Izzi Dien is of Iraqi origin and has a doctorate in Islamic law from Manchester University. He currently lectures at St David's University College, Wales, where his subjects include amongst others Islamic law and Religion and the Environment. He has also written a book on the environment and was for ten years assistant professor at King Abdul Aziz University in Jeddah, Saudi Arabia. Othman Llewellyn is an American and works as an engineer for the National Institute for the Environment in Saudi Arabia. Al-Hafiz B. A. Masri was born in India and is an environmentalist, author and broadcaster. He was the first Sunni Muslim to be appointed Imam of the Shah Jehan mosque, Woking, Surrey, and since his retirement in 1968 he has dedicated his time to animal welfare and the environment. He is the founder of the Muslim Association for Animals and Nature and has written two books on the care and protection of animals from a Muslim perspective. Yunus Negus was born in Kent, England, and has a doctorate in zoology and a master's degree in computer science. He now lectures at Newman-Westhill Colleges, University of Birmingham. Umar Ibrahim Vadillo is a Basque from northern Spain. He is now part of the growing community of Muslims in Granada, Spain, and has made a special study of Islamic trading systems. The editor of this book is a Sri Lankan by birth and has lived in England for the past 40 years. He has worked for 25 years in race and community relations, much of which has been spent with community groups and young people. He is now a management consultant and also a consultant on Islam for the Religion and Conservation network of the World Wide Fund for Nature.

My thanks are also due to Joanne O'Brien, my co-editor. Without her support this book would have been a near to impossible task in what has been for me an intense period of activity. And to the World Wide Fund for Nature UK and the International Consultancy on Religion, Education and Culture for presenting me with this opportunity. My thanks are also due to Saba, my wife, for being available to test ideas, for her helpful suggestions, for her patience and her support, and to the children, Batool and Samya. My prayer on behalf of the team that helped to produce this book is that we leave a world as beautiful and worthwhile to live in for our children and theirs as our parents and grandparents left for us.

Fazlun M. Khalid
Birmingham, August 1991

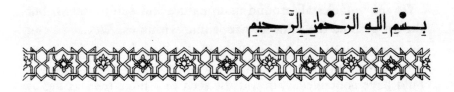

1 ‖ ISLAM AND ECOLOGY

Al-Hafiz B. A. Masri

INTRODUCTION

There are so many stars and planets in the heavens that it is impossible to count them. Yet, in all those heavenly bodies we have not been able to find anything that has life, except on our planet Earth. Even here there are so many different species of living creatures and animals that it is impossible to count their classes. Yet, out of these millions of kinds of living beings, we are the only species who have the brains to understand the difference between right and wrong in the moral sense and who can use the power of our minds to choose between the two.

It is only because of this freedom of choice that we are considered to be higher in rank than the other animals. Animals, too, possess minds and can distinguish between what is good or bad. However, their brains are not developed enough to distinguish between virtue and sin. Our freedom of choice, based on knowledge and intelligence, puts on us the added responsibility of caring for the rest of God's creation and for those very resources of nature which help all kinds of life on earth to stay alive.

1

We see miracles all around us in nature and admire them, but take for granted the miracles happening within us. We see an egg and wonder how it could contain in it a huge bird, as big as an ostrich. We watch a seed grow and wonder at how that little acorn could have contained within it the seed of a huge tree, as big as an oak. But have you ever given serious thought to the miracle of your own birth? How a tiny baby—a helpless lump of flesh and bones—contained your full-grown muscular body and an intelligent brain which would one day be capable of controlling the forces of nature—and, we hope, managing to do so more wisely than your forefathers have done. The Qur'an draws our attention to these miracles in these words:

> It is God who creates you weak as babes; then after weakness, gives you the vigour of youth; and again, after a phase of strength, He ordains senility as your lot with hoary hair . . .
>
> (Qur'an 30:54)

> It is God who causes the seed-grain and the fruit-kernel to split and sprout. It is He who brings forth the living from the dead; and the dead too from the living. How is it, then, that you are still in a delusion?
>
> (Qur'an 6:95)

> Has not there been a time in a man's life when he was not a thing worth mentioning?
>
> (Qur'an 76:1)

> He creates man out of a mere drop of fluid; and Lo! this same being grows up into an open rebel.
>
> (Qur'an 16:4)

There are about 500 such verses in the Qur'an giving us guidance on matters relating to the environment and how to deal with it. There are, however, some people who think that these problems can best be solved by scientists, economists and other learned people and that Islam is meant to give us guidance only on spiritual matters. But Islam does not make this distinction between the spiritual and the physical well-being of humanity. When dealing with humanity and ecology we cannot ignore the other species that inhabit the earth. We tend to forget that all living creatures, including human beings, are subject to the same laws of nature. Our planet is the only one in the whole universe known so far to be capable of supporting life. Perhaps it is wishful thinking but if there are other planets in the universe with life on them, one hopes that their inhabitants are wiser than us and that they do not go around cutting the very branches of the tree of life on which they are sitting.

Although the Qur'an describes humanity as being created in the best forms, it also tells us in the same verse that some people degrade themselves to the lowest of low positions (Qur'an 95:4, 5).

THE PLANET EARTH

Until a few centuries ago it was believed that the space on earth was limitless and that its resources were endless. This wrong impression gave people the idea that they could go on using up and wasting its means of supplying their needs as they liked, without exhausting them. Unfortunately, in spite of our knowledge of the limits of the earth's resources, we continue to behave in the same way.

It is estimated by some leading cosmologists that the earth is about 4,600 million years old. Its total land area is 329 million hectares out of which only 226 million hectares are available for use. The remaining 103 million are either barren, or cannot be reached, or are unsuitable for agriculture. Nearly three-quarters of the earth's surface is covered by water, 98 per cent of which is sea water and salty and 1 per cent of which is in the form of ice in the Antarctic and Arctic regions. Thus, 99 per cent of the earth's water cannot be used directly for human needs. It is on only 1 per cent of the total supply of water that all the living creatures of the world depend. These figures could be misleading without mentioning that the existing 226 million hectares of land and 1 per cent of water are diminishing fast because of our wasteful and unwise ways of using them. There are vast areas of usable land which are turning into deserts or are being flooded. For example, the latest research shows that the present area of usable land in the Northern

3

hemisphere will diminish from 25 per cent to only 1 per cent at the present rate.[1]

There are repeated warnings in the Qur'an about this. For example:

> Nay, We let them and their forebears enjoy the good things of life, until they outlive their prosperity. Can they not see that We visit the land under their control and gradually curtail its boundaries all around them. Is it, then, they who will prevail?
>
> (Qur'an 21:44)

One of the main causes of our ecological problems is our refusal to accept hard facts in the light of the fresh knowledge that we have started gaining. The information we were given in our early scriptures on the creation of humanity and the earth has either been misunderstood or has been wilfully misinterpreted. We flatter ourselves by continuing to behave as though we are the only creatures for whom all this universe has been created and as if our earth is the centre of the cosmos. The real fact is that humanity is just one of the millions of other species inhabiting and sharing this earth with us.

When the famous Italian astronomer Galileo invented a telescope through which the other heavenly bodies could be seen more clearly, the Church was against him. They thought that this discovery would demolish the theory of the earth being the centre of the universe. Today we know that the 'earth is merely the third-rate planet of a fourth-rate sun which, with other planets, forms an insignificant unit in a vast galaxy, which in turn is only one out of countless galaxies'.[2]

There are many theories as to how this whole universe came about. Some are mere suppositions while others claim to be based on astronomical science. One such theory is that originally space did not exist and then, over 15,000 million years ago, a loud explosion occurred and heavenly bodies started being formed. This theory is called the 'Big Bang' theory. According to it, one such heavenly body named Earth gradually developed in such a way that life became possible on it.

Scientifically it is true that the universe could not have come into existence without the forces of gravitation and expansion.

These forces have been arranged in all the heavenly bodies with absolute perfection and proportion. It is this arrangement that has made it possible for billions of bodies in the cosmos to go on moving precisely in their fixed orbits. Even a slight variation in it would create chaos and confusion in the ordered system of the universe called the cosmos.

The Qur'an does not disagree with such scientific theories as far as the laws of nature are concerned, which it tells us are uniform, constant and run according to rules. However, it does not agree with the scientists on certain points which are very important and have a great bearing upon man's mental attitude towards nature and, hence, upon his behaviour towards ecology. It rejects the idea that the laws of nature were devised by nature itself. On the contrary, they have been laid down and are enforced by the Supreme Controller we call God (Allah in Arabic). The universe is His scheme; He knows what is needed to run this universe and weighs and measures everything accordingly. The Qur'an tells us, for example:

> Have they never cast a glance at the firmament above? How We have set it up and decked it out! And how there are no rifts in it. And the earth—We have spread it out like a carpet; have cast on it firm mountains and caused it to grow, in pairs, all kinds of palatable vegetation.—All this merits deep reflection and reminiscence by every penitent votary.
>
> (Qur'an 50:6–8)

> God is He who has raised up the heavenly canopy without any visible support. Then He established Himself on the throne of authority and made the sun and the moon subservient to His laws—each orbiting its course according to its appointed term. He it is who regulates the cosmic affairs and explains clearly His portents, so that you may be convinced of your eventual meeting with Him—by reflecting on these phenomena.
>
> (Qur'an 13:2)

> It is He who created the heavens and the earth, according to a plan and with a purpose. Whatever He wills to 'Be', it evolves into 'Being'—His words turn into reality.
>
> (Qur'an 6:73)

5

It is not entirely clear what scientists mean by 'Big Bang', and it is interesting to note that new scientific evidence has recently emerged which suggests that this theory may have been wrong from the very beginning. According to the Qur'an, the universe, including the earth, was created gradually in six aeons, meaning six ages of the universe or six stages:

> Have not the incredulous people considered that the heavens and the earth were originally one closed up mass, and We rent them asunder? Do not they know that it is out of water that We have made everything living? Will they not then give credence to Our portents?
>
> (Qur'an 21:30)

> To Him is due the primal origin of the heavens and the earth. When He creates a thing, He has just to say to it to 'Be' and it evolves into 'Being'.
>
> (Qur'an 2:117)

The ecological problems we are facing today arise from the fact that we have started using very scarce resources wastefully and in such a way that we are not giving nature a chance to reproduce the things we are taking out of it. We are also consuming non-renewable resources at a very fast rate. The laws of nature are based on its own rhythm; we must learn to operate in accordance with that rhythm.

When we study the lives of early Muslims, we find that they considered all the elements of nature as the common property of all the creatures. Our right to use the natural resources is only in the sense of usufruct—which means being given the right to use another person's property on the understanding that we will not damage, destroy or waste what is in our trust. According to Islamic law the elements of nature such as land, water, air, fire, forests, sunlight etc. were considered to be the common property of all—not only of all human beings, but of all creatures. The Islamic juristic rules and legal principles on this issue are very specific and clear—based on the Qur'an and Hadith, such as:

> Ask then: 'To whom does the earth and all that it contains belong, if you know'.
>
> (Qur'an 23:84)

... Surely the earth belongs to God, and He bequeaths it to such of His servants as He pleases ...

(Qur'an 7:129)

Certainly, to Him belongs all that the heavens and the earth contain ...

(Qur'an 22:64)

This is what an early Muslim legal scholar, Abu al-Faraj, says:

People do not in fact own things, for the real owner is their Creator; they only enjoy the usufruct of things, subject to the Divine Law.

Then the Qur'an tells us how to use the resources:

Eat and drink, but waste not by indulging in excesses; surely, God does not approve of the intemperate.

(Qur'an 7:31)

The Holy Prophet (S), sets the standard by which the usage of a thing should be judged with these words:

The merit of utilization lies in the benefit it yields, in proportion to its harm.

(Tirmidhi)

CORRUPTION

Modern scientific findings leave no doubt in our minds that everything on earth, in space and in time, is interwoven into a beautiful and extremely intricate and complicated balance of nature. This balance is particularly important in the case of the earth which is, perhaps, the only living planet in the universe. The Qur'an repeatedly tells us to maintain that balance and not to upset the order in nature. It tells us again and again that this world has not come about just as a result of some freak accident:

Know that We did not create the heavens and the earth, and all that is between them, in frivolous play. Had We wished to indulge in a pastime, We would have found the means at hand—as if We would ever be indulging in that kind of amusement.

(Qur'an 21:16, 17)

7

We created man and gave him the faculty of speech. The sun and the moon rotate in ordered orbits, the plants and the trees, too, do obeisance. The firmament—He raised it high, and set the balance of everything, so that you (humanity) may not upset the balance. Keep the balance with equity, and fall not short in it.

(Qur'an 55:3–9)

Do they not learn a lesson from the chronicles of history; and see they not how many a nation we have made extinct in the past? They were the people whom We had established on earth even with more power and prosperity than We have established you. We had showered on them both the celestial bliss and the earthly affluence. Yet, when they became iniquitous, We toppled them down and raised new civilizations in their wake.

(Qur'an 6:6)

Don't you see that it is God who has created the heavens and the earth, not without a plan and purpose? He can, if He so wills, remove you and put in your place a new people. That will not be so difficult for God to do.

(Qur'an 14:19–20; see also 46:3; 15:85, 86)

Let us see how humanity has been breaking the Covenant with God and ignoring His warnings. A study of history shows that humans have in many instances been exploiting the resources of nature carelessly to satisfy their needs, even those which are not really necessary. Other species also use the resources of nature for their needs, but they use them in a sustainable way—that is, in such a way that nature can replace what is used. According to this verse, animals have understood the laws of nature and obey them more than humans.

Seest thou that unto Allah pay adoration all things that are in the heavens and on earth—the sun, the moon, the stars, the mountains, the trees, the animals, and a large number among mankind. However, there are many humans who do not, and deserve chastisement.

(Qur'an 22:18)

Perhaps the following verse contains a prophecy, foretelling the corruption which God knew would take place on a large scale. The Qur'an was revealed some 1,400 years ago and at that time there was not even a fraction of the kind of corruption which has started taking place in our time. We have done more damage to the environment during this century than had been done since the beginning of the world:

> Corruption has appeared over land and water on account of what man's hands have wrought.

(Qur'an 30:41)

POLLUTION

Let us see how this prophecy about corruption is being fulfilled in our time and how, and on what scale, humanity has started causing ruin and destruction on earth.

Water

Every day some 25,000 people contract illnesses from bad water because two-thirds of the people on earth have no choice but to drink it, cook with it and bathe in it. A total of 20 billion tons of unclean water flows every year from lakes and rivers to our oceans. This water is polluted and poisoned by sewage, agricultural run-off and industrial wastes. One third of rain water on land flows back to the sea. Rivers and streams have no boundaries, therefore one country's polluted water may be another country's drinking water. Some 40 per cent of the world's population depends on water from a neighbouring country.[3]

Water is a big divide between the rich and the poor. There is more water in the Northern hemisphere of the globe than there is in the Southern hemisphere. The range of use varies from up to 20,000 litres per capita a year in the United States of America to less than 500 litres in some developing countries.[4]

1,200 million people, mostly in rural communities, use unsafe water. The waters of almost all the rivers in the world, especially those in developing countries, have become polluted. Since many pollutants have no distinctive colour or smell, it is not easy for an average person to judge from the look of water whether or not it is safe.

In the light of these facts and figures, plus the fact that our earth is the only planet in the universe known so far to contain water, it is not surprising that the Qur'an lays so much emphasis on the importance of water. Here are just a few such verses:

> God created every animal out of water: of them there are some that creep on their bellies; others that walk on two legs; and others on four. . .
>
> (Qur'an 24:45)

> It is he who has given the free flow to two kinds of water—the one thirst-quenching and sweet, and the other salt and bitter. Yet, He has set an insuperable barrier between their intrinsic qualities which cannot be changed. It is He who created man out of the very water and, then, established his relationship of kin and wedlock.
>
> (Qur'an 25:53, 54)

Air

> It is God who looses the winds that set the clouds in motion, and We drive them on to a land that is dead. Thus do we bring back the earth to life after it has been dead. . .
>
> (Qur'an 35:9; see also 30:48, 49)

Are the winds bringing with them these days the Grace of God, or poison? Are they setting in motion the clouds to shower on us the gift of life, or acid rain? Humans are sending up to ten times as much gas into the air as volcanoes and forest fires ever did. There is hardly any clean air anywhere, not even in Antarctica or in the highest mountains.[5]

Scientists tell us that they have not yet been able to find out how long it takes the air and water to recover from these toxic effects. According to the World Wide Fund for Nature, 'the combined effects from emissions we pump out hang invisibly in the atmosphere and refuse to disperse'. We are sending up into the atmosphere so many harmful gases that nature cannot cope with them all. The massive emission of gases such as carbon dioxide, methane and chlorofluorocarbons has led to a thickening of the barrier of gases that hang in the earth's atmosphere. The resulting global warming has led to what we call the 'Greenhouse effect'.

Leading scientists are now predicting that over the next 50 years the earth's average temperature could rise by 4 degrees Celsius. Even this small rise could cause the polar ice to melt and the oceans to rise; low-lying coastal areas and small islands would be submerged. The impact of global warming and changes in the seasons is bound to be disastrous not only to human beings but to all sorts of life on earth, including plants and trees. We have already started having droughts, storms, shortages in water supplies, and breakdown of the whole chain of life on land and in water.

Forests

Trees cover a third of our earth. They regulate climate, protect water supplies, nurture millions of species of animals. They soak up carbon dioxide and other gases and, therefore, maintain a natural balance in the world's temperature and climate. Half of our medicines are derived from plants. Out of 3,000 plants from which medicines for cancer and other diseases are made, more than 2,000 come from the Amazon rainforest. By destroying the rainforest, we will never know what useful plants we may have lost. The area of the world's tropical rainforest that is being destroyed in Africa, Asia and Central and South America is estimated at about 14–20 million hectares every year. Even in Europe, which has a total forest area of 141 million hectares, 50 million have been damaged by acid rain.[6]

Forests are being cut for timber or to provide extra land for cultivation. Large areas are being cleared to be turned into pastures for cattle in order to export their meat to meet the demand of other countries. It is only the trunks of trees that can be used as timber; their twigs and debris are left to rot, releasing carbon dioxide and methane into the atmosphere.

The situation has recently become so desperate that the United Nations Environment Programme, working closely with other United Nations agencies and international environmental organiz-

11

ations, called for 8 billion dollars to be spent on the Tropical Forestry Plan during the five years ending 1991.

The Islamic legislation on the preservation of trees and plants, laid down some fourteen centuries ago, covers not only forests but also wildlife. According to these laws, certain areas, called *harim* or *hima*, are set aside and development or cultivation is prohibited. This code of ecological legislation was based on numerous verses of the Qur'an and sayings of the Holy Prophet Muhammad (S). They include the following:

> The world is green and beautiful and God has appointed you as His stewards over it. He sees how you acquit yourselves.
>
> (Muslim)

> Whoever plants a tree and looks after it with care, until it matures and becomes productive, will be rewarded in the Hereafter.
>
> (Bukhari and Muslim)

> If anyone plants a tree or sows a field and men, beasts, or birds eat from it, he should consider it as a charity on his part.
>
> (Imam Ahmad, Musnad)

The Qur'an repeatedly draws our attention to the fact that even plants and trees are 'living beings', by pointing out that they too have been created in pairs as male and female. Like human beings and animals, they too are meant to go on reproducing themselves and keep their species going:

> My Lord is He who spread out for you the earth like a carpet; and made paths therein for you, and sent down water from the clouds. Then, thereby, We have produced diverse pairs of plants, each distinct from the other.
>
> (Qur'an 20:53)

When the Holy Prophet Muhammad (S) became the ruler of Makkah and Madina, he declared the trees in and around these cities as protected by decrees such as:

> I declare Madina to be sacrosanct throughout the area between its two mountain paths, so that. . . leaves may not be eaten off them except for fodder.
>
> (*Mishkat al-Masabih*)

> The game in Makkah is not to be molested, nor its fresh herbage cut.
>
> *(Mishkat al-Masabih)*

These laws were enforced by a decree that the tools of the person who cuts trees shall be confiscated and shall become the property of the person who catches the culprit.

Early Muslims understood and respected these decrees. After the death of the Holy Prophet (S), Hazrat Abu Bakr succeeded him as the first Caliph in 632 CE. Before sending an expedition for a battle to a place named Muta he gave his troops some instructions, including the following concerning trees and animals:

> Do not cut down trees and do not kill animals except for food (in the enemy territory).
>
> (Tabari, Exegesis of the Qur'an)

In later years, Muslim law-makers based the Islamic legal system on such decrees and formulated similar laws covering the conservation of forests, over-grazing, water resources, animal rights etc. They even formulated laws hundreds of years ago to hold in check over-population in cities—a problem which has now become a major cause of ecological disaster throughout the world. In Africa, for example, the number of people coming to live in cities is growing at the rate of 4 per cent a year. It is estimated that between 1980 and 2000, 200 million more people will have moved into cities.

Owing to the Qur'anic influence and the interest aroused by the Islamic laws on animals and the environment, Muslim scholars and naturalists were prompted to do research in these fields. As early as the eighth century CE one such scholar, Al-Jahiz, wrote *The Book of Animals*. In this book he discusses animal behaviour and suggests that a change in the environment could bring about a gradual change in their character and behaviour. It is interesting to note that Darwin (1809–1882 CE) reached similar conclusions around a thousand years later. It must be mentioned, however, that Darwin did not agree with Al-Jahiz that this evolutionary process takes place according to a well-planned pattern and a purpose set by the Creator of the universe.

13

Another similar example is that of the famous Muslim legal scholar, Izzad-Din Ibn 'Abd As-Salam. As early as the thirteenth century CE, he formulated a 'Bill of Animal Rights' (see p. 91). Unfortunately, the early Islamic literature on such humanitarian subjects is not widely known by Muslims today. There is little or no mention of such works in school or university textbooks. One seldom hears our teachers speaking on these subjects in their discourses and sermons.

ECOLOGY AND ANIMALS

The pressure of human need

God's guidance on humanity's relationship with other species is quite comprehensive. It would need a lengthy book to deal with it properly and the following short discussion is only meant to give a few examples of the Islamic laws that apply to our relationship with other living species.

It would seem that we are universally shirking our responsibilities towards animals. The real reason behind our uncaring attitude is our selfishness. Giving the other species their due share according to their rights demands some sacrifices on our part—which we are not prepared to make. Our short-sighted self-indulgence does not permit us even to understand the simple fact that our own well-being is interwoven with the well-being of all other creatures on earth. This is how the Holy Prophet Muhammad (S) puts this simple truth:

> Whoever is kind to the creatures of God, is kind to himself.[7]

One of the main reasons why human beings are becoming increasingly aggressive towards animals is the increase in our needs. Apart from the fact that our present lifestyle is creating more and more artificial needs, there are more mouths to feed in this century than ever before. United Nations statistics show that 'the world's population reached 5.3 billion in 1990, and is expected to reach 6.3 billion by the year 2000 CE. About 93 per cent of the extra one billion people will be in developing countries.'[8]

There is no doubt that there are more and more mouths to feed, but this is no place to enter into the controversial question of family planning or birth control, except to suggest that the problem needs to be studied afresh from the non-materialist point of view as people of faith. Allah has promised to provide sustenance for every mouth He creates. The following verses of the Qur'an support this position:

> He is the Sustainer of the heavens and the earth, and of all that lies in between them—if you could but have firm faith.
>
> (Qur'an 44:7)

> Ask them: 'Who is it that provides you with sustenance out of the heavens and from here below . . .'
>
> (Qur'an 10:31)

But Allah also makes it clear that humans will have to earn their bread by the sweat of their brows; that a person's share shall be in proportion to his or her labour; and that God knows best as to who deserves how much. The following verses apply equally to individuals as well as to nations:

> Man shall have nothing, but what he strives for.
>
> (Qur'an 53:39)

> God bestowed His blessing on the earth, and measured therein sustenance in due proportion . . . in accordance with the needs of those who seek.
>
> (Qur'an 41:10)

> Verily! your Sustainer augments or circumscribes the means of sustenance for whomsoever He pleases—for He knows and keeps a watchful eye on all His creatures.
>
> (Qur'an 17:30)

> Gracious is God to His men. He provides sustenance to whomsoever He pleases—for He is All-Powerful, All-Mighty!
>
> (Qur'an 42:19)

What these and numerous other similar verses on this theme are trying to explain to us is that God is the Sustainer—but not in the sense that He pushes morsels of food down our throats. He is the Sustainer in the sense that he has equipped the earth with all the

15

necessary ingredients to sustain life; and it is up to us to produce our food in a sensible way. It is only then that God has promised to give us our 'share in proportion to what we have earned through our labour, in accordance to our needs'. He, at the same time, warns us that we should 'have nothing unless we seek and strive for it'. Are we doing that in a sensible way?

The outbreak of famine in various parts of the world is more to do with the fact that we have broken the rules of nature than with over-population. We have polluted our land, water and air and have, therefore, broken the natural chain of our food supplies. Agricultural experts would verify that this planet is capable of sustaining four times more people than the present population, if only we would work and manage more diligently and sensibly.

The current use of agricultural land does not make any economic sense. More than 80 per cent of the earth's arable land is used for producing fodder for cattle. We need 100 acres of fertile land to pasture enough animals to feed 20 people. The same 100 acres could produce enough maize to feed 100 people, or wheat to feed 240 people, or beans to feed 610 people. In Great Britain, for example, we consume about 450 million animals every year. To feed these animals we import cereals from the same underdeveloped world where people are constantly undernourished and even dying of starvation. All this absurd waste is going on in spite of modern scientific evidence that the human body could derive all its nourishment from a fibrous and mixed vegetarian diet.

The relationship between people and animals

In the current scramble for food, it is the animals who have started to pay the price of human mistakes. We have started killing them to the point of extinction. Instead of killing them singly, as used to be done, modern technology has put in our hands tools to kill hundreds of them at one go. For example, nylon drift-nets with a 13-mile span can sweep the oceans like a vacuum cleaner, killing anything that comes their way whether it is edible or not.

In order to produce food-animals faster and more cheaply, we have started rearing them intensively, tightly packed together in windowless sheds or factory farms. Dairy cows are now bred and fed scientifically to yield many times more milk, thus reducing their productive lives by about three years. Their calves are taken from them at two or three days old, artificially fed and then sold, mostly to veal farmers. Many of these veal farmers put these calves into narrow crates until they are ready for slaughter at about four months old. Throughout this period, these innocent young animals are unable to walk or even turn around. An honest farmer would tell you that calves are highly sociable animals, but their crates are designed so that they cannot even touch or see each other.

Battery hens are being treated in more or less the same manner. They are packed tightly into wire cages and kept there all their productive lives, crouching on a wire floor. The wing span of a battery hen is about 80 cm, yet five or six of them are usually crowded into a cage 50 cm wide. Throughout their lives they are never given a chance to express their natural and inherited behaviour.

It is not only in the name of human need for food that we kill animals, but we also kill them needlessly for trinkets and fancy goods. The carnage of animals such as elephants, rhinos, whales, crocodiles, seals, and numerous others has led to the near-extinction of many such species. Millions of animals are tortured and killed under the pretext of scientific experiment, although most of these are experiments for commercial enterprises—for example, the supply of cosmetics—for which alternatives are readily available.

We rear animals in barbaric ways supposedly to improve the quality of their meat or we encourage animals to fight with each other or with humans in the name of sport. Bullfights, the chase, badger-baiting and falconry are considered legitimate sports. One could carry on giving examples of the inhumanity of human beings, for it is forgotten by many that we are meant to be God's stewards on earth.

Animals are generally held in contempt by humans, largely because they are considered to be dumb. We behave towards them as though they had no feelings, and often degrade them or treat them badly. The Qur'an and Hadith remind us that they are communities like the human community; that they are loved by

17

God in the same way as human beings are loved; that they were created the same way as we were; that they are as much a symbol of God's power of creation as human beings are. See how the following verses make these points clear:

> There is not an animal on earth, nor a bird that flies on its wings, but they are communities like you . . .
>
> (Qur'an 6:38)

> All creatures are like a family (*ayal*) of God: and He loves the most those who are the most beneficent to His family.
>
> (Shu'ab al-Imam)

The Holy Prophet (S) told his companions that a Prophet in the olden days was stung by an ant and ordered the whole of the ants' nest to be burnt. At this, God reprimanded him in these words:

> Because one ant stung you, you burned a whole community that glorified Me.
>
> (Bukhari and Muslim)

Note the equality of treatment suggested between man and beast in this hadith:

> A good deed done to a beast is as good as doing good to a human being; while an act of cruelty to a beast is as bad as an act of cruelty to a human being.
>
> (*Mishkat al-Masabih*)

Some of the companions of the Holy Prophet (S) snatched at the young ones in the nest of a bird called in Arabic *hammarah*. When the Prophet (S) saw the mother bird hovering above in grief he asked 'Who has hurt the feelings of this bird by taking her young?' and ordered them to return the fledglings to the nest. It says in the Qur'an:

Do you not see that it is God whose praises are celebrated by all beings in the heavens and on earth, even by the birds in their flocks? Each creature knows its prayer and psalm—and so does God know what they are doing. And yet, you understand not how they declare His Glory.

(Qur'an 24:41)

Do they not observe the birds above them—spreading their wings out and closing them? None save the Merciful God can uphold them there—for verily! He keeps all in sight.

(Qur'an 67:19)

These days, with the advance of science, we know that animals and birds communicate with each other. The Qur'an told us so some fourteen centuries ago:

Solomon was David's heir, and he said: Lo, my people! we have been taught the speech of birds and have been given the abundance of all good things—this indeed is a distinct favour on us.

(Qur'an 27:16)

In the verse that follows, we are told that God spoke even to the bees:

And your Lord revealed to the bees: Make hives in the mountains, and in the trees, and in human habitations.

(Qur'an 16:68)

In this verse, the Qur'an puts the human species in the same class as the other species, by describing man as a two-legged animal:

Allah has created every animal from water: of them there are some that creep on their bellies; some that walk on two legs; and some that walk on four . . .

(Qur'an 24:45)

19

THE ROLE OF MANKIND

Since the beginning of recorded history, Prophets have been lay-ing down guidelines for us about how to lead a happy, healthy and useful life in this world—useful not only to us but also to every-one and everything on earth. Muslims say the following prayer many times during their five daily prayers:

> Our Lord! Give us the best of this world
> as well as the best in the Hereafter.

The Holy Prophet (S) advises us:

> Live in this world as if you were going to live for ever; prepare for
> the next world as if you were going to die tomorrow.
>
> (Bukhari)

Islam teaches us not only to achieve personal piety but also how to conduct this earthly life. In order to have a broad understanding of life on earth, it is necessary to understand and respect the laws of nature as laid down by the Creator of this universe. Any activity that has social implications or effects on others must con-form to the physical laws of nature as well as to the moral and ethical discipline laid down by the Creator. We cannot escape the fact that the human species is just one of the millions of species inhabiting the planet. Each individual and each species is a part of life as a whole.

It is we, the human species, who are responsible for the ecologi-cal problems and it is up to us to solve them. Laws and regulations passed by a government are obeyed, whether or not all people agree with them. Often people break such laws when they think they will not be caught. Laws laid down by the Creator, on the other hand, are accepted by our free will. The worldly-wise experts can help us with facts and figures, but it is faith that can bring about within us a change of heart and a revolution in thought. The most important factor is a complete change in our character—in the way we think and act. Islam is a complete way of life. If we sincerely believe this, then we should be applying our faith as much to our practical conduct of this worldly life as we apply it to our personal piety. In the words of our Holy Prophet (S),

> A true believer is one who does not hurt others with his thoughts, words or actions.
>
> (Bukhari)

If we believed that this world is the 'be all and end all' of our existence, our actions would be guided by selfishness. It is this kind of attitude which has led to most of the present ecological corruption, human misery and degradation of animals. The Qur'an describes the attitude of such people and nations in these words:

> There are some people whose views on worldly life may sound convincing to you, especially when they justify themselves by quoting alleged testimonials of God in support of their views; while, in fact, they are the most contentious kind of adversaries. No sooner do they come to power, after leaving you, than they hasten to go about the earth spreading corruption and destroying the flora and fauna [vegetation and animal life]. God does not approve of corruption; and when they are told to fear God, their vanity takes the better of them. Such people end up with a life in hell—What a miserable end!
>
> (Qur'an 2:204–206)

God is the Supreme Controller of the Universe and it is He who has created it, including our planet Earth, for a purpose which He knows best. He has created each and every living being, including humans and animals. He has been sending His messengers from time to time to give us guidance and to help us in the development of our souls, which do not die at the time of our physical death. When our souls are presented to Him, He will judge us as to how we conducted ourselves during our lives on earth. Most importantly, He is a personal God—full of mercy and concern for each individual being. One of the things on which we shall be judged by God is the active kindness we are expected to show to all that He has created, as we are told by the Holy Prophet Muhammad (S) in these words:

21

> All creation is like a family of God; and He loves the most those who are the most beneficent to His family.
>
> *(Mishkat al-Masabih)*

God is not someone who lives somewhere remote in the heavens. He is always here with us and can be approached by each of us, as the Qur'an tells us:

> When My devotees enquire of you about Me, tell them I am indeed near at hand; I respond to the call of every suppliant when he calls Me.
>
> (Qur'an 2:186)

> Your Lord says: 'Call Me, and I shall answer . . .'
>
> (Qur'an 40:60)

> It is We who created man, and We know what dark suggestions his mind makes to him—for We are nearer to him than his jugular vein.
>
> (Qur'an 50:16)

The answer to all our problems on earth lies in humanity's total submission to the will of this kind of God, and in trying to carry out His will which He expresses through the laws of nature. That is what the Qur'an tells us in these words:

> Set your face to the true religion—the nature of God on which He has instituted the innate nature of mankind. No change is permissible in God's creation. This is the eternal religion.
>
> (Qur'an 30:30)

Let us try to grasp the true spirit of the eternal word of the Creator before it is too late.

References

1 *Our Planet*, the magazine of the United Nations Environment Programme (UNEP), 1990 and 1991.
2 C. E. Last, *Man in the Universe*, Werner Laurie, London, 1954.
3 These figures are based on the findings of the United Nations Global Environment (UNGE) programme: *Our Planet*, 1991.
4 Dr Malin Falkenmark, *Case Studies in Population and Natural Resources*, World Conservation Union and IUCN, 1990.
5 *Outreach* (UNEP), no. 59, part 4, 1990, pp. 2–6.
6 UNGE (see 3 above), p. 3.
7 Muhammad Amin, *Wisdom of the Prophet Muhammad*, Lion Press, Lahore, Pakistan, 1945.
8 *Our Planet*, vol. 3, no. 2, 1991, p. 12.

بِسْمِ اللَّهِ الرَّحْمَنِ الرَّحِيمِ

2 | ISLAMIC ETHICS AND THE ENVIRONMENT

Mawil Y. Izzi Dien

BASICS OF ETHICS AND SHARI'AH

One of the major problems in our society is caused by the fact that the motive for good behaviour is often confused. In other words, nowadays many people do not know the difference between what is ethical and what is not.

Ethics according to Shari'ah is a state, *hay'a*, that resides in our souls. All voluntary actions, be they good or bad, beautiful or ugly, are based upon it. This state is influenced by upbringing, for upbringing can lead to the perception and admiration of virtue. The continuation of a good upbringing usually leads this hay'a to the love of good and the hatred of evil. This is known in Arabic as *khuluq hasan* or good ethics. Bad upbringing or bad ethics, *aklaq sayi'a*, would lead to the opposite. Islam strongly recommends good ethics just as it denounces the bad. Allah described the Prophet of Islam (S) as a person who has great ethics:

> And lo! thou art of a tremendous nature.

> (Qur'an 68:4)

The source of Islam's ethical obligations can be deduced by reference to the Qur'an which, while describing the human soul, tells us that the soul has been given within its creation its state of feeling for good or evil:

> And a soul and Him Who perfected it
> And inspired it (with conscience of) what is wrong for it and (what is) right for it.

(Qur'an 91:7, 8)

Human beings have been provided with various talents among which are knowledge and the different instincts; a sense of ethics has also been given to them:

> Oh, but man is a telling witness against himself,
> Although he tender his excuses.

(Qur'an 75:14)

They have been guided to both the good and the evil path:

> Did We not assign unto him two eyes
> And a tongue and two lips,
> And guide him to the parting of the mountain ways?

(Qur'an 90:8–10)

The soul can order evil, but human will can control this evil tendency:

> But as for him who feared to stand before his lord
> and restrained his soul from lust,
> Lo! the Garden will be his home.

(Qur'an 79:40)

The story of Abu Hanifa's father reflects how much good ethical awareness is respected in Islam. He was walking by a stream when he saw a fig floating by. Being hungry he picked up the fig and ate it. After eating it he remembered that the fig might belong to someone else. He followed the flow upstream and found that it led him to a plantation of figs. The owner of the plantation told him he would not accept any money for the fig that he had eaten without permission. Rather, the price he asked was for him to marry his blind and dumb daughter. The God-fearing man had to accept in order to clear his conscience. After he married her he discovered her to be most beautiful and completely healthy, with all her faculties intact. Abu Hanifa's father asked his new father-in-law why he had lied. The man replied, 'I did not lie. I told you the truth in a different way, because I wanted a man of great character to marry my daughter. She is dumb since she has never heard nor spoken evil, while she is blind because she has never seen evil.'

WHY HUMAN APPOINTMENT?

Human beings are the only creatures with the special qualities that enable them to serve the earth. One of these qualities is the ethical notion which leads them to care about their environment. Other qualities include the knowledge given to them in order that they might perfect their duties.

The following verse describes how and why humankind was given the ability to know the names of creation, which is an important symbol of knowledge, unique to the human race from among all other creatures, including the angels:

> And He taught Adam all the names, then showed them to the angels, saying: Inform me of the names of these if ye are truthful.
>
> (Qur'an 2:31)

The ability to name that which he sees around him is of great value to man. Without this ability, life becomes a great mystery and all matters can easily become bewildering and confusing. A mountain can be identified only if a coding word is available, without this special word it can be a hill or even a valley. The angels, which are another kind of creature, were asked to do the same as Adam. Their answer was:

> ...Be glorified! We have no knowledge saving that which Thou has taught us. Lo! Thou, only Thou, art the Knower, the Wise.
>
> (Qur'an 2:32)

God's response was to demonstrate to the angels the powers that we humans were given by him, and indeed it is a demonstration to us as well:

27

> He said: O Adam! Inform them of their names, and when he had informed them of their names, He said: Did I not tell you that I know the secret of the heavens and the earth? And I know that which ye disclose and that which ye hide.
>
> (Qur'an 2:33)

After Adam had displayed the knowledge which Allah had granted him, the angels were ordered to prostrate themselves before him. This they did. The prostration of the angels to the first human illustrates the dignity which humankind possesses, even though they corrupt the earth and shed blood. Humankind was granted a position above the angels, and was given the secret of knowledge and an independent will which permits them to choose their own way. The duality of our nature—the ability to pave our own way together with the duty of viceregency—is the reason for our dignity. This ability of humankind which is unique to them puts the surrounding creation in a very different position if humans do not do what is right for them. Having placed us on earth and given us the duty of operating the life-support system, Allah decided that this fantastic creature needed a manual to operate the magnificent system properly, or at least to operate that part of the complex cosmic system relevant to it. Humankind was given the different instructions, which evolved according to their need; the Islamic law or Shari'ah was the latest such updated manual.

THE 'NATIONS' OF ALLAH

Islam acknowledges that humans are not the only creatures that are worthy of protection and cherishing. All that God has created are 'nations' or 'communities' similar to that of the humans:

> There is not an animal in the earth nor a flying creature flying on two wings but they are nations like unto you. We have neglected nothing in the Book (of our decrees). Then unto their Lord they will be gathered.
>
> (Qur'an 6:38)

Muhammad (S) is reported to have said:

> All creatures are God's dependants and the most beloved to God, among them, is he who does good to God's dependants.
>
> *(Kashf al-Khafa')*

This saying demonstrates the strong value that Islam gives to caring for the other members of our environment. Muhammad (S) is also reported to have said:

> The most perfect of the believers is he with the most perfect character.
>
> *(Kashf al-Khafa')*

The Prophet of Islam (S), who is described by the Qur'an as a person of great character, is reported to have said about the mountain of Uhud, close to Makka:

> It is a mountain that loves us and we love it.
>
> (Bukhari)

This love, according to Ibn Hajar al-Asqalani quoting various Muslim scholars, is explained in various ways. One is that the Prophet (S) loved the people of Madina who supported him and lived near Uhud. Another explanation for the Prophet's (S) love for the mountain is that it is an actual love for one of God's creations. The Prophet (S) was also reported to have spoken to the mountain when it was shaken by an earthquake, saying to it:

> Be calm, Uhud!
>
> (Bukhari)

Human love for the elements of the environment symbolizes the utmost in caring relationships which can be learnt from the man who had such a great character. That same love extends to other elements of the environment, including living creatures which inhabit this world with us and which were made by the same creator—Allah. Allah has enacted upon us humans certain obligations towards other living creatures. We will be responsible on the Day of Judgement for how we have treated these creatures, and it is advisable for all of us to bear this in mind. The owner of an animal is obliged to feed it and to treat it if it is ill. This is because the Prophet Muhammad (S) said:

29

> Allah punished a woman because she imprisoned a cat until it died of hunger. She neither fed it, nor let it obtain its own food.
>
> *(Riyadh as Salihin)*

No one should over-burden an animal, for Allah forbids man to treat an animal in a way which would cause it unnecessary pain. Every animal is protected by Allah and the person who violates this protection violates the order of Allah. A man cannot even milk an animal at a time or in a way which would damage its young. This is because the milk belongs to the young animal. Moreover, before a Muslim comes to milk a cow, he is expected to cut his nails so that he does not unwittingly hurt her. Likewise, when honey is taken from a beehive, enough should be left for the bees' own use.

The protection of Islam for animals extends beyond mere physical protection for it goes so far as to prevent the cursing of an animal. Ahmad and Muslim have transmitted a hadith, narrated by Imran, in which the Prophet Muhammad (S) overheard while travelling a woman cursing a female camel. He reprimanded her, saying, 'Leave it alone' (without) being cursed.

PUBLIC DUTIES TOWARDS THE ENVIRONMENT

Public duties are one subject that any legal system may find difficult to control or legislate upon. Often the problem is due to the changeable character of these duties. Although they can be given a general definition and many of them specified, public duties have proved difficult to stipulate. In today's society some selfish people reject the whole notion of caring for others let alone their environment. For Muslims selfishness has no place, it is quite clear that all is for one and one is for all. The Prophet of Islam (S) likened the attitude of Muslims towards their society to that of the body: if any part of it suffers, all the rest feel the pain.

The Islamic ethical attitude towards the environment is greatly affected by the fact that Islam is not only a set of beliefs or dogma, it is a way of life, *manhaj hayat* (as Sayyid Qutub, the great twentieth-century scholar, summed it up). Islam came to reassert belief in the one God but also explicitly to create a new community (*ummah*) of individuals who would be better human beings, who look to God and who accept moral and ethical codes and follow rules of behaviour. These rules cover all the actions that either are expected to be practised by the member of society or from which he should refrain. Significantly, duties do not have to be described by the law since they form part of the general Islamic ethical manner.

The foundation of the Muslim community occurred in the 23 years between Muhammad's (S) proclamation of his mission and his death. During these years the doctrine was stated, the form of worship prescribed and the community built up. The basics, the details of Muslim law and the Muslim code of behaviour, were laid down. This behaviour did not only focus on general social conduct, it also paid great attention to small personal matters. A smile can be seen as fresh air. The importance of this simple act was emphasized by Muhammad (S) when he said:

> Smiling in the face of your brethren is a charity.
>
> (Tirmidhi)

Muhammad (S) also told Muslims to beware of sitting in the streets. The Muslims said that the streets were where they met and talked. The Prophet (S) replied that they should give the road its duty. They asked what was the road's duty? The Prophet (S) replied:

> Removing mischief, casting the eyes down and ordering good and prohibiting evil.
>
> (Muslim)

PRACTISING GOOD AND PROHIBITING EVIL

Good is called in Arabic *al-ma'ruf*, which means the good prevalent practice, be it at an individual level or in society. It is a word which is mentioned in the Qur'an 39 times. All Muslims are expected to practise the ma'ruf in all aspects of their lives. Another part of a Muslim's duty is to oppose all kinds of evil. The main religious foundation for public good deeds is the Qur'anic injunction:

> Let there be from among you a group of people who order the good—*ma'ruf*, and prohibit the evil—*munkar*.
>
> (Qur'an 3:104)

A hadith emphasizes this:

> Anyone who witnesses evil should remonstrate upon it by his hand, his mouth, or his heart, the last is the weakest of faith.
>
> (Imam Ahmad, Musnad)

Both the Qur'an and the Hadith indicate that *hisba*, the application of good and removal of evil, should be exercised with the full intention that it is only for the sake of God, and accordingly such actions will be added to the good deeds of the person who executes them. This notion of public responsibility started in the form of individual concerns about the righteousness of the community. Thus if a man encounters a wrong deed he should try to correct it as best he can. As Muhammad (S) was walking in the market of Madina he saw a man selling dates. The prophet placed his hand in the pile of dates, discovering that it was wet and going bad underneath:

> 'What is this?' the prophet enquired.
> 'It has been affected by the rain', the man replied.
> 'You should expose it for everyone to see. He who cheats is not from among us'.
>
> (Muslim)

Obviously the Prophet Muhammad (S) was very interested in developing public morality, replacing a predatory society of individuals with a disciplined community of sociable human beings with a collective tendency.

The action of hisba or ordering good and prohibiting evil can be practised by either a volunteer or an appointed person, either a man or a woman. The volunteer is called *muhtasib mutatawi'*, and any member of Muslim society can perform this task so long as he does so meritoriously and has the relevant knowledge of Islamic principles. Mutawi today is the surname of a prominent Arab family. *Al-mutawi'* is also the name given to those who supervise the eradication of vice and application of good in Saudi Arabia. Unfortunately, in practice this institution is now limited to the very restricted area of making sure that Muslims pray at the proper time. The main reason for this is its confinement to the service of Islamic ritual, while it is in reality a supervisory watchdog meant for all avenues of life.

The Muhtasib in the community

Knowledge is a necessary requirement since a person given this power might interfere with what he should not, or even worse give a wrong order. The appointed muhtasib is in a stronger position than the volunteer by virtue of his appointment. The individual form of action remains valid but branched (about the second century AH/eighth century AD) and fossilized into concentration on the market, although it is still capable of supervising all human activity. With the growing complexity of society and the development of various trades and markets the institution of hisba became even more distinct. By the fourth century AH/tenth century CE the muhtasib had become one of the top officials of the state. He, through his various juniors, controlled the mint, and supervised the Caliph's flags and uniforms, as well as taking care of the market and preventing fraud. During the tenth century the hisba system was established in Egypt and from there it spread to North Africa. The multiplicity of duties and responsibilities invested in the muhtasib, especially in metropolitan areas, made the prestige of the post almost equal to that of *qadi* (judge).

Caring for the environment falls within the jurisdiction of the muhtasib, and such care is expected from a Muslim during his daily life. Water should not be wasted; remember *wudu* (ablution or ritual cleansing with water) is the ultimate symbolic action that the Muslim performs every time he prepares himself for prayer. Water therefore is one of the main sources of purity and life. It should not be wasted even when it is used to prepare for prayer, according to the tradition of the Prophet of Islam (S). Next to water in purity is earth. If no water is available then earth should be used, for the Prophet of Islam (S) followed the Qur'anic order and practised *tayamum*. This is performed by rubbing the hands on clean earth and wiping the face and arms with it.

Caring for life and its elements is not only a peace-time practice. During war this care is expected to extend even further. The Muslim army has its own muhtasib to make sure that:

> Trees are not burnt, nor unjustifiably pulled out and that women, children, the elderly and unoffending priests or monks should not be harmed. He also ascertains that water and medicine are given to the prisoners of war.

> (*Al-Taratib al-Idariyya*)

Coming back to times of peace we find another interesting area of the muhtasib's responsibilities: public health. We know from history that he and his inspectors fought a continuous battle to keep the streets clean, at least in the more important parts of town. Moreover because the importance of clean food and drink in the prevention of disease was discovered by Muslim scientists, the ordinances governing the provision of food and drink were severe and the muhtasib enforced them strictly.

The muhtasib had more responsibility and power than the Greek *agoranomos* or today's trading standards officers. He made sure not only that the market place was clean, but that trading was honest and people's behaviour decent. The muhtasib also ensured that all slaughtering was performed hygienically in a slaughter-house and, perhaps more importantly, in a merciful way.

From these rules hisba might seem like a Weights and Measures Act. This might be true, but the greatest advantage of hisba is its ability to apply justice in a very swift, ethical, and practical manner rather than becoming involved in the complexity of the law.

Public duties in Islam are seen as a part of the general meritorious and ethical tendency of the faith. In this way many problems in society today can be dealt with through the application of hisba. The environment is a good example: if Muslims were to feel that they were responsible for its protection as a part of their religious and ethical duty, then hopefully future generations would not have to live on a polluted and mutated earth.

Bibliography

Abd al-Hayy al-Kittani, *Al-Taratib al-Idariyya*, Rabat, 1346 AH.

Ibn Hajar al Asqalani, *Fath al Bari*, Madina, 1379 AH.

Ismail ibn Muhammad al-Ajluni, *Kashf al-Khafa' wa Muzil al-Ilbas*, ed. A. al-Qallash, Damascus, 1983.

Abu Bakr al-Jazari, *Minhaj al-Muslim*, Jeddah, 1985.

Imam al Nawawi, *Riyadh as Salihin*, ed. M. N. al Albani, Damascus, 1984.

Muhammad M. Pickthall, *The Glorious Qur'an, Text and Explanatory Translation*, Karachi.

Al Hasiz Al Mudhiri, *Mukhtasar Sahih Muslim*, ed. M. N. Albani, Kuwait, 1979, p. 134.

بِسْمِ اللّٰهِ الرَّحْمٰنِ الرَّحِيمِ

3 | SCIENCE WITHIN ISLAM
Learning how to care
for our world

Yunus Negus

FIRST UNDERSTAND ISLAM, THEN UNDERSTAND SCIENCE

Islam is the religion of oneness. This is because it is based upon a simple but amazingly powerful truth: that there is no god except the One True God, who is known in Arabic as Allah. Allah is the Creator of the whole universe. He also looks after everything in the universe and controls the universe through His eternal commands. Nothing can escape His commands. The Qur'an repeatedly says: 'Allah has power over all things'. Muslims believe that the Qur'an is the actual words spoken by Allah, and conveyed to His Messenger Muhammad (S), by the angel Gabriel.

The Qur'an tells us that everything that Allah has created in the universe completely submits to His will. So a rock is perfectly the rock that Allah commands it to be, the tree is exactly what Allah commands it to be, and wild animals such as the deer, the camel or the tiger are all exactly as Allah wishes them to be. Everything in creation is obedient to Allah in this way, no matter whether it is non-living like the air, the earth or the oceans, or living, like the animals, the plants, the bacteria and the fungi. It makes no difference whether something is microscopic or immense. The particles of atoms and the massive galaxies of outer space are all obedient. And because each thing that Allah created is exactly as He wishes it to be, then everything in creation works properly and the whole creation fits together in a meaningful way. Creation is therefore sacred. The Prophet Muhammad (S) said: 'The whole of this earth is a mosque', that is, a place of worship.

Each thing that Allah has created 'praises Him' just by being a perfect creation in itself. So, when we see a beautiful mountain, or the sun glittering on the sea, or a beautiful tiger, then each of these, through its sheer beauty, is praising Allah. Of course, not everything is physically beautiful, but everything which Allah has created praises Him in some way or other, not necessarily because it is beautiful but because it is faithful to the will of its Creator. So everything created is like a faithful Muslim:

> All that is in the heavens and the earth praises Allah, the Sovereign, the Holy, the Mighty, the Wise.

> (Qur'an 62:1)

> Do you not see that all things bow down to Allah, all things in the heavens and in the earth, the sun, the moon, the stars, the hills, the animals; and a great number of mankind?

> (Qur'an 22:18)

THE 'SIGNS' OF THE CREATOR

Nature also reveals to us some of the wisdom of Allah. The Qur'an tells us that:

> Surely in the creation of the heavens and the earth and in the alternation of the night and of the day are signs for men possessed of minds who remember Allah.

> (Qur'an 3:190)

> The ship that runs in the sea with profit for man, and the water Allah sends down from the sky with which to revive the earth after it is dead ... and the turning about of the winds and clouds com-

pelled between sky and earth—surely these are signs for a people having understanding.

(Qur'an 2:164)

We can see from these quotations that Allah speaks of all existing things in His creation as well as some of the objects such as ships that are built by man, as 'signs' of their Creator. This means that the universe and everything in it is a system of design. It is produced by an infinitely intelligent designer and programmer, who 'writes' His wisdom into His creations in such a way that He can ask us to remember Him whenever we see them. This means that the study of the universe and what exists in it is an important way of studying the wisdom of Allah. Since science is nothing else but the study of the universe, then this means that the duty of scientists is firstly to try to understand and secondly to reveal for mankind the wonderful order and intelligence of the universe. It is important however to remember that the Qur'an warns us that even when the signs of the Creator are pointed out there will be some men and women who refuse to believe.

The title of this chapter is 'Science *within* Islam'. The words were chosen deliberately to make the point that there are in fact two kinds of science. One is based on nothing else but human thought and the belief that the physical universe is the only reality. This kind of science does not include any idea of the unseen spiritual world, nor does it accept the afterlife. It is basically atheistic and is outside of Islam. It seeks to prove that the universe came into being without a supernatural cause and that human beings have arisen merely by chance. The science that is *within* Islam differs from this because it always starts with the view of the world given in the Qur'an. This is because the Qur'an contains complete truths which are not necessarily obvious to the human mind. The Qur'an says that Allah:

taught man what he [that is, man] did not know.

(Qur'an 96:5)

The starting point for science within Islam is that the universe was brought into being by Allah from nothing. It originates simply from the free will of Allah to create and from His choice to

39

create this particular universe with all its unique features and laws. The Muslim scientist is not therefore concerned with the origin or cause of existence, he already knows that all things have their origin in Allah. However the Qur'an does not merely say that Allah is the Creator, it also gives us a broad idea of the ways in which Allah has created. The Qur'an says:

> He is Allah, the Creator (*Khaliq*), the Bringer-into-Existence (*Bari'*), the One-who-gives-physical-form (*Musawwir*).
>
> (Qur'an 59:24)

Khaliq is the Divine Name that describes Allah when He freely chose to create either the whole universe or just a single being within it. *Bari'* is Allah when he acted to give a thing a separate existence, and finally *Musawwir* is Allah when He gives to the created thing every detail of its complicated spiritual and physical existence, and ensures that it fits perfectly into the rest of His creation. It is very clear that the Qur'an teaches us the doctrine of creation. We do not know how Allah created but we know that He did. In fact, if you think about it, there is no possible way in which the Creator, who has the power to create from nothing, could possibly explain to man, who is one of His creations, how He did it.

THE METHODS OF SCIENCE

Science involves a way of working that makes it possible for us to learn more about the created universe. It is a way by which the 'Book' of creation can be opened, explored and deeply appreciated. Science is about understanding and whenever we begin to understand something we must have a starting point. For Muslims the starting point is simply that the universe is the creation of Allah and nothing in the universe has an origin except from Him. To make it possible for us to understand His creation Allah has given us three kinds of guidance. These, in order of importance are: firstly, Revelation through the Qur'an, which is absolute truth; secondly, the gift of human intelligence and, thirdly, the gift of the human instincts. Intelligence should be guided by Revelation, and instinct should be guided by intelligence. As a result both intelligence and instinct can be guided by Allah. Science, then, which is method that uses the intelligence, must be guided by the Qur'an, otherwise it risks being lost in a wilderness of opinion, theory and error. Scientists should realize from the outset that they can never discover the secret of the origin of existence since scientific methods of investigation cannot probe into the secrets of Allah.

There are two methods that are used in science. One is called *observational* science. It consists of making a number of careful observations and then analysing them to see if it is possible to detect a meaningful pattern. The pattern may allow the scientist to make a prediction. When further observations are made it may be that the prediction is seen to be true. This is the kind of science that is of great importance in detecting changes in the environment, especially long-term changes such as climatic variation, or the decline or increase of animal and plant populations.

The second method is called *experimental* science. This kind of science also begins with observation and interpretation, but then goes on to develop a hypothesis, which is a kind of prediction that can be tested by means of an experiment. In an experiment the scientist tries to bring about a single, isolated change in whatever he is observing, while measuring some other single, isolated change. For example, he or she may treat different plots within a field with different quantities of water and then measure the mass of the crop produced from each plot. In that case the hypothesis might be that 'there is a certain amount of water needed for the greatest production of crop'. The experiment is designed to find out exactly the amount of water required. In another experiment the scientist may measure the maximum load that a bridge of different lengths can support. In each case the scientist seeks to discover a link between the thing he or she changes, such as the bridge's length, and the thing measured, such as the load the bridge can hold before breaking. Muslim scientists would say that they are doing experiments like these to discover something about the 'nature' (*tabi'ah*) of an object or of a system that Allah either has created Himself or has made it possible for man to construct. Of course, Allah created both the materials that man uses to make

41

things and also the natural laws that he discovers, even though man makes use of them for his own purposes. The Qur'an reminds us:

> Is it not His [i.e. Allah's] to create and to govern?
>
> (Qur'an 7:54)

The major difference between Western and Islamic science is that Western scientists invent theories from their observations and experiments that completely ignore Allah. They attempt to explain physical existence in terms of nothing else but physical existence. Theories such as Darwin's Theory of Evolution or the Big Bang origin of the universe are alien to Islam, because they are explanations which exclude Allah and moreover have no basis in the Qur'an. It is true to say, however, that a few Muslim scientists have mistakenly tried to find evidence in the Qur'an of ideas belonging to twentieth-century Western science. This is not a wise thing to do because one of the things about Western science is that the theories are always open to rejection or change. So a Muslim who tries to find evidence of such ideas in the Qur'an might have to think again in a hundred years' time. Apart from anything else, it seems a mistake to impose ideas that arise out of human experience upon the eternal words that come from Allah.

Muslim scientists explain the 'natures' of created things in terms of their supernatural origin. This also helps to emphasize the sacred character of creation, since to abuse what is natural, or to show lack of respect for nature, is to show lack of respect for the Creator.

THE USES OF SCIENCE

The study of science must fit into Islamic education as a whole. Education is concerned with developing in an individual a system of beliefs and values and helping him or her build up a sound view of his or her life. It is also concerned with the imparting of knowledge about creation that encourages admiration for the Creator and promotes an understanding of the need for care and respect whenever the resources of creation are made use of for the benefit of man. Traditionally Islam distinguishes between education for an individual, and education for society as a whole. Islam also distinguishes between what is essential for every individual to know and what is necessary for only some to know. Traditionally a study of the natural sciences falls into the second category. This is because the good of the whole community will be served so long as an adequate number of students study science. However the Qur'an, as we have already seen, encourages us to observe and try to understand the 'signs' of the Creator. Moreover, nowadays it is common for all students to study science at some time during their lives. So it seems that a science that consists of a 'study of the signs of Allah' is a source of knowledge suitable for all Muslim students. Al-Ghazzali (died 1111 CE), an important writer on theology, mysticism and education, wrote that

> The knowledge you acquire must reform your heart and purify your soul.

Another important consequence of knowledge is that it must result in useful action. Knowledge must not be amassed for its own sake, it is then simply a waste of precious time and resources. So, if science is to be studied then both the teacher and the student should fully understand the reason and the application of the topic. There are two general reasons for the study of science. One is based upon the duty to meditate upon the perfection that is present in creation. The Qur'an says:

> Thou seest not in the creation of the All-Merciful any imperfection. Return thy gaze; seest thou any fissure? Then return thy gaze, and again, and thy gaze comes back to thee dazed, aweary.

> (Qur'an 67:3–4)

The essential thing about appreciating perfection through a study of science is that perfection must never be attributed to the thing itself. The result of understanding perfection should always be to praise the Creator. The second reason for the study of science is to enable mankind to make use of some of the materials and forces of nature for the benefit of all. This use of knowledge is called technology; it has always been associated with science.

SCIENCE MUST HELP US PROTECT THE ENVIRONMENT

There is a major problem with technology. An ancient Chinese sage called Cheung Tzu is said to have seen a farmer using a hand-operated machine to irrigate his land; the sage remarked to the farmer: 'If you do not destroy that device it will eventually cause you famine and will destroy you'. The point that is being made here is not that technology is bad in itself, but that it is so very easy for it to be misused. Perhaps the worst aspects of technology are that it can be used to make some people rich and powerful at the expense of others, and that its use can seriously damage the natural environment. We live in a world that has learnt, through painful experience, that life on this earth, both human and non-human, is threatened by technology.

Technology exists as soon as someone picks up a stone axe and starts to cut down trees, or makes a plough and begins to till the soil. Technology has brought benefit but also many problems. This is because it too often takes selfish short cuts that seriously disturb the natural environment. Part of the solution to the problem lies in understanding the role of man in the world. Islam describes man as the *khalifah*. This means that man as the 'vice-regent' of Allah on earth has the duty of looking after the earth which has been entrusted to his hands. It is an enormous responsibility since man must eventually give an account of his stewardship of the resources of the planet. The Qur'an relates that when Allah announced to the angels that He was:

> about to create a viceregent in the earth, they said: Wilt Thou place therein one who will do harm therein, and will shed blood?

> (Qur'an 2:30)

The special gifts that man has, that make him different from all other creatures, can so easily be used for destruction.

It is obviously essential that there should be great emphasis on the scientific study of every detail of natural systems and of the effects of human technology upon them. Students need to include such studies in their science education. It is equally important for scientists to make proposals for ways in which the resources of the earth, which have been given to us by Allah, should be used with minimum disturbance to the environment and maximum concern for the maintenance of harmony and equilibrium. The fundamental rule that is taught to us by the above quotation from the Qur'an is that we should *expect* that every new technology is likely to have a damaging effect upon the planet. It may be that a particular effect is small and the natural ecological systems can respond sufficiently well to cope with the effect. On the other hand it may be that the effects are so great, or so prolonged, that such technologies should never be developed. The problem is that man is so confident of himself that often only the advantages are considered, very rarely the disadvantages. But for such short-sighted developments the price to be paid may eventually be serious damage to the earth.

The Shari'ah or Law of Islam distinguishes between five kinds of acts which can apply to science as much as to anything else. These are: *halal* (approved), *mandub* (recommended), *mubah* (indifferent), *makruh* (reprehensible) and *haram* (forbidden). As a result of the unrestrained use of technologies that belong to the categories of makruh or haram we are nowadays faced with the extinction of many species of plants and animals, the destruction of forests, the poisoning of the oceans and the catastrophes arising from the warming of the planet. In fact the effects of technology are so great that scientific studies can hardly keep up. Seyyed Hossein Nasr, in his book *The Encounter of Man and Nature*, suggests that one reason why the development of technology came to an end in Islam in the Middle Ages was an awareness that there was a threat to the natural environment.

Science and technology have a complicated influence upon one another, while at the same time having lives of their own. Neither however can be allowed to operate in an uncontrolled and independent way. Professor Nasseef of King Abdulaziz University, Jeddah, writes that a 'crucial problem is the control of science'. He suggests that the following four types of thinking need to be built into science education:

1 Studies of societies that make students aware of the damaging effects science may have on a community.
2 Studies of the environment that increase students' awareness of the impact of science and technology on the natural environment.
3 Studies of the whole world that inform students about the problems that can arise from the action of science and technology on world development, especially where it leads to unemployment and exploitation by a power-elite.
4 Religious studies from which students may learn 'how the knowledge that science imparts should be organized so that man may acquire power for the benefit and peace and happiness of mankind, how man can grow up and behave as the viceregent of God on earth'.

The importance of these four topic areas is that they prepare us in advance for the inevitable problems that will arise as soon as new technology becomes available. The fourth topic gives us a positive view of science and technology, but emphasizes that we must always promote science and technology within the context of religion, not separately, as if science were its own master.

ISLAMIC SCIENCE AND THE MUSLIM SCIENTIST

Seyyed Hossein Nasr's book *Islamic Science: An Illustrated Study*, which is an excellent resource for teachers and students, argues that Islamic science is really different from Western science. Western science pretends that it is free of beliefs and values, although many authors, including Nasr, have shown us that a science that has no values is impossible. Science within Islam has never pretended to be free of values. In fact, its distinct character is precisely because it arose in the value system of the Shari'ah of Islam. The Shari'ah, being the system of laws and morals for the community, states and enforces what is correct for the community. It takes as its standard the Qur'an and the Sunna. The science that arose in Islam was therefore neither independent of the needs of the community, nor disobedient to the will of Allah. The greatest development of Islamic science took place during the tenth and eleventh centuries CE. In the twelfth and thirteenth centuries CE almost all the written works describing advances in subjects like mathematics, medicine, astronomy and physics were translated into Latin in Sicily and Toledo and then made use of by European scholars. After that Islamic science seems to have faded away.

Islamic science was just one part of a complicated set of studies. The Muslim scientist was a *hakim*, that is a wise man who was competent in many subjects such as languages, astronomy, medicine and theology. Above all else he was a Muslim believer, who used his intelligence for the pursuit of truth and wisdom. Western science during the last 600 years has gradually separated itself as a self-contained subject. It has dismissed many parts of human experience as 'unscientific' and has declared itself to be independent of values and beliefs. We are beginning to see some of the consequences of this mistaken philosophy world-wide. As Professor Nasseef says:

> The great disparity we notice today between technological achievement on the one hand and ethical behaviour on the other can only be removed if science education is controlled and directed towards findings and activity ultimately beneficial for mankind and for his environment.

To conclude this chapter and to sum up the main points that we have discussed, it would perhaps be useful to list some of the thoughts that should guide a Muslim student in his or her study of science. The most important thing about such thoughts or ideas is that they should produce a unity between the student's religious practice and his or her education in science. Good ways of thinking and good attitudes will have a positive effect upon the quality of work done by the student. Good ideas and attitudes will also increase the student's admiration and respect for creation. Such students will become good and helpful members of a community of believers that will treat the environment and all living things with love, care and gratitude.

Here is a list of four such ideas or concepts:

47

1 The immense complexity, the enormous size and the minute details of the universe all have their origin and inner meaning in the One Creator, Allah. Our Creator, although hidden from us is also, as He tells us in the Qur'an, amazingly close. He says:

> We are nearer to you than your jugular vein.
>
> (Qur'an 50:16).

2 The creation of the whole universe has its origin in the 'absolute goodness' of Allah, which is expressed by His Name *al-Rahman*, which means 'the Beneficent', or 'He who Actively Does Good'. It is because of His Beneficence that creations can be perfect in themselves and can act in sympathy with everything else. This is why it is possible for life to exist and for complicated ecosystems to be self-contained, self-regulating and full of wisdom for their survival. It is also the reason why natural beauty can exist. The Qur'an says:

> The Beneficent, He taught the Qur'an, He created mankind, He taught him understanding and speech. The sun and the moon glorify Him, the stars and the trees prostrate before Him.
>
> (Qur'an 55:1–6)

3 All created things, both living and non-living, have an orderly existence, which makes it possible for all the details about them to be understood by scientists. Things also behave according to 'laws' which it is possible for us to understand. The order that created things possess comes from the original command (*amr*) of Allah, when He created each of them, and to the determining power (*gadr*) of Allah who controls their existence. So when a scientist formulates a law of motion, or describes the control systems within a living cell, he reveals details of the order that Allah commands for His creation.

4 Mankind has a responsible and God-given role to play in creation. He is the khalifah, the one who holds the earth in trust. Allah has provided guidance that enables man to distinguish between those acts that are haram or forbidden, because they are destructive and an offence to Allah, and those acts that are halal and are approved of by Allah. These principles must guide every aspect of the life of man, including the life of communities and the way in which they make use of the resources of the

world. In his care for the natural environment man must be resolute in refusing to do things that are haram, that is forbidden, even though the gains that could be made seem to be very tempting. Often he must be prepared to take the harder path. For a Muslim student the challenge to conserve and protect the world is very similar to the duty to protect and conserve his or her own soul.

A short resource list

Seyyed Hossein Nasr, *Islamic Science: An Illustrated Study*, World of Islam Publishing Company, London, 1976.

Seyyed Hossein Nasr, *The Encounter of Man and Nature*, Allen and Unwin, London, 1978.

Seyyed Hossein Nasr, *Science and Civilization in Islam*, Islamic Texts Society, Cambridge, 1987.

(Nasr's books make up a mine of information and thought. They are very demanding for the younger student. Perhaps the illustrated study would be the most useful as a first study resource. Nasr always presents the spiritual dimension in his books.)

Abdullah Omar Nasseef and Paul J. Black, *Science Education and Religious Values*, The Islamic Academy, Cambridge, 1984.

(This is a short booklet containing two articles, one from a Muslim and one from a Christian point of view. There is a short introduction by Syed Ali Ashraf.)

Ziauddin Sardar (ed.), *The Touch of Midas: Science Values and Environment in Islam and the West*, Manchester University Press, 1984.

(This book is a useful resource of thirteen separate articles. It includes aspects of the history of science in Islam, the thoughts of some modern Muslim scientists and a comparison between Western and Islamic attitudes.)

4 | NATURAL RESOURCES IN ISLAM

Yassin Dutton

OWNERSHIP AND SHARING

The main principles and precepts in Islam concerning the earth's natural resources are dealt with in this section. Of these resources land and water are the most important since they form the necessary basic elements for all human life and activity. We shall consider these two first, and then turn to a consideration of the animal, plant and mineral resources which are supported by or derived from them.

LAND

In terms of use, Islamic law divides land into three main categories: developed (*amir*) land, undeveloped (*mawat*) land, and 'protective zones' (*harim*). The word amir comes from an Arabic root meaning 'alive', the word mawat comes from an Arabic root meaning 'dead' and the word harim comes from an Arabic root

51

meaning 'forbidden'. This means that the use of harim land is forbidden to anyone but the owner.

Developed lands include any place where there is human settlement and/or agricultural activity, whether this is a huge metropolis or a little homestead with an associated field in the middle of a wilderness. Undeveloped lands are those which are neither settled by humans nor being cultivated, i.e. rough grazing land and wilderness areas. The third category, harim lands, are those areas which act as a protective zone around developed land, protecting the development and ensuring access to it.

Developed lands

Developed lands are of two types:

1 Those whose owners are known, and about which the government has no say, except to collect the *zakat*. Zakat is an obligatory annual tax on wealth above a certain minimum level (known as the *nisab*).
2 Those whose owners are not known, which includes land set aside by the government from conquered territory for the benefit of the whole community, which belongs to the people and so can be hired out but not given away, and land that reverts to the government if the owner dies without an heir.

Undeveloped lands

The basic rule is that undeveloped or mawat land belongs to whoever 'brings it to life', i.e. puts it to use and develops it, either by building on it or cultivating it. All the main manuals of Islamic law contain sections on what is known as 'bringing dead lands to life' (*ihya al-mawat*), which means developing undeveloped lands. Development in this sense is considered to have taken place when undeveloped land is 'brought to life' in one of the following ways:

— by putting a hedge or wall around the land in question;
— by irrigating the land (if it is too dry) or draining it (if it is too wet);
— by digging a well or creating a spring;

— by clearing the area of trees, breaking up stones, and levelling the ground;
— by tilling or ploughing the land;
— by planting crops or trees on it;
— by erecting a building on it.

Development in this way brings with it rights of ownership, on the basis of the hadith of the Prophet (S): 'If someone brings a dead piece of land (mawat) to life, it is his', with the condition that 'an unjust root has no right'. An 'unjust root' is whatever is dug, taken, or planted without any right to do so (Imam Malik, *Muwatta*).

Mawat land can be developed either by private initiative with or without permission from the government (according to a difference of opinion on this point) or when such land is assigned to an individual by the government, when it is known as *iqta*. Mawat lands can also be set aside by the government as a *hima*, or specially protected area (see pp. 54–6).

Harim lands

Associated with all developed lands is a third category, the harim, or protective zone. Such land shares characteristics with both developed and undeveloped land. In terms of usage it is undeveloped, like mawat land, but, unlike mawat land, which is not owned, harim land is always owned by the owner of the developed land with which it is associated.

Every development, whether it be a well, or a house, or a field full of crops, has its associated harim, or protective zone, and this zone necessarily varies in size. Around a town, for instance, the harim is traditionally defined as that area which can be reached and returned from in the same day for the purposes of collecting fuel and/or pasturing livestock. For a source of water, whether a well, spring or river, it is that area around the water which enables access to it by both people and livestock without causing either overcrowding, or damage to other people's land, or pollution of the water itself. For crops and trees, etc., it is the area that is necessary for their roots to obtain sufficient water and also to enable the owner to have access, for example paths between properties.

The important distinction here is that undeveloped land is not owned by anyone but is held in common, although the government may administer it for the public good, whereas developed land and its associated harim zone is always owned, even though it may be a general ownership, as in the case of harim lands around a village where the villagers have rights to fuel and pasture.

Himas

A hima is an area of undeveloped or mawat land that has been set aside to remain as mawat land in order to protect pasture, etc. Such land cannot then be developed and must remain as mawat land in perpetuity, although there is a difference of opinion on this point. A hima can be created by the government on public lands or by an individual on his own land.

This concept of the hima is interesting in that it is one of the practices current in Arabia in the time before Islam which were then adopted and developed by the Muslim community because they were of benefit to the community and did not contradict any of the fundamental principles or precepts of Islam. There was one necessary change, however, with the hima: in the period before Islam a chief could declare a whole area of public mawat land as a hima for his own personal use, whereas in Islam it is only possible to do so 'for Allah and His Messenger' (al-Mawardi), which means that it can only be set aside either for the general benefit of the community or specifically for those in need amongst them: it can never be set aside solely for the rich, for example. The Prophet Himself (S) set aside an area around Madina of one mile by six miles as a hima for the horses used in war, and this practice was continued by the Caliphs immediately after him: Abu Bakr, the first Caliph, set aside an area near ar-Rabadha as a hima for the animals collected as zakat, and Umar, the second Caliph, set aside a similar area of land for animals to be used by the army at ash-Sharaf. (Madina, ar-Rabadha and ash-Sharaf are all places in present-day Saudi Arabia.)

Use of public land can thus be restricted by the government by the creation of a hima, but this must be done with justice, i.e. when there is a genuine need, and as long as the area that is set aside is not so large that it would cause hardship to others. Thus it is not permissible to set aside all the undeveloped lands of a community since that would be unjust (in restricting the development of new areas for agriculture and settlement, etc.). Furthermore, the government may not make any charge for the use of such himas, since the Prophet (S) said:

> All the community are equal partners in three things: water, fire and pasture.
>
> (al-Mawardi)

Himas today

It is interesting to note that this concept of the hima still survives today in the Arabian peninsula, though now they are more usually akin to village harim lands than areas set aside by a Muslim government. There were an estimated 3,000 himas in Saudi Arabia alone in 1965, with more than 30 in the Taif area, although this number must certainly have declined since then.

There are various restrictions on the use of such village himas; five main types have been recorded:

1 where grazing is prohibited, but grass cutting for fodder is permitted in years of drought;
2 where grazing and cutting are permitted on a seasonal basis;
3 where grazing is allowed but restricted to certain numbers and/ or kinds of stock;
4 where the area is kept primarily for bee-keeping, with no grazing allowed during the flowering season;
5 where the area is primarily to protect trees, with cutting either prohibited or restricted.

The administration of these himas is usually the responsibility of the local village or tribe, with decisions on how they should be used being taken by the local headman, or *shaykh*. He is the one who decides when the hima is to be opened for grazing, for how long, and for what kinds or quantity of livestock. Furthermore, although usage of such himas is normally restricted to the local tribe, the shaykh may permit other tribes to use his own tribe's hima or himas, in times of special need.

It is thus clear that this system is very flexible and can readily be adapted to the needs of a particular community. It is this flexibility, and the similarity of the concept of a hima to that of a reserve, that has led many authors to remark on the great conservation potential of himas, not only as a means of ensuring sustainable rangeland management, but also for creating wildlife reserves and wilderness areas, etc. They have particular value for:

— allowing the rehabilitation of degraded rangeland, or its maintenance where it is not degraded;
— preserving the diversity of plant species for better quality and more varied pasture;
— preserving the genetic diversity of individual plant species (which has important economic implications);
— producing plants for human use (for food, fibres, fuel, etc.);
— protecting watersheds and water catchment areas;
— providing living-space for wildlife, and thus also for a valuable economic resource;
— providing a potential tourist attraction.

The main distinction in Islamic land law is thus between what is public and what is private. This distinction is important because land that is owned privately may be bought, sold, given away and inherited, etc., by the owner as well as used by the owner provided he or she does not cause harm to others in so doing, since a basic principle of Islam is that one should neither cause harm to others nor reciprocate it. Where land is not owned by individuals, however, there is open access for all, unless such land becomes private either by government assignation (iqta), or by being developed (ihya), or where there is a restriction on access under the hima system.

We may also note that this division of lands into developed and undeveloped contains a four-way pattern of land-use. Developed lands, or what we could call the 'human environment', consist firstly of human dwellings—cities, towns, villages, etc.—which are primarily the domain of people, and, secondly, agricultural lands, which are primarily the domain of crops. Undeveloped lands, or what we could call the 'natural environment', consist on the one hand of rough pasture and grazing, which is primarily the domain of livestock, and, beyond that, the wilderness areas— mountains, forests, deserts, etc.—which are primarily the domain of wild animals. In the first category, the 'human environment', the land is owned, and the owner has his or her rights. They can use land as they choose, provided this use does not harm others, and, because such land is owned, it can be bought, sold, given away and inherited, etc. In the second category, the 'natural environment', the land is now owned by many individuals and everyone has an equal right to its use (except that the state may set aside some of it as a hima for a specific benefit to the community, as we have seen). This is because of the hadith already mentioned, that: 'All the community are equal partners in three things: water, fire and pasture'—i.e. water for both man and his livestock and crops; firewood and fuel for himself; and pasture for his livestock.

WATER

Water in its natural state in public (mawat) lands is considered common property, as we have seen from the above hadith. There are, however, clear principles for determining priority of usage.

Water resources are classified in Islamic law into three main categories: rivers, wells and springs.

Rivers

Rivers are divided into three categories:

(A) Large naturally-occurring rivers, where the water is permanent. These may freely be used by anybody for watering live-stock, irrigating land, etc., and channels may be dug from them.

(B) Small naturally-occurring rivers. These are of two types:

57

1 those which contain enough water for the needs of the local people, in which case channels may be dug to take the water further away, providing no harm is done by this to the local people (e.g. depriving them of their water);
2 those which contain insufficient water for local needs unless they are dammed, in which case the people furthest upstream have the prior right, then those next downstream, and so on. This rule is based on a judgement of the Prophet (S) regarding the flood channels of Mazhur and Mudhaynib in Madina, where the water was to be retained until it reached ankle-depth and then released for use by those next downstream, and so on. This of course was a specific judgement for a specific situation: the principle is that there should be a just division of water, which depends on the following five factors, which necessarily vary from place to place:

— the type of soil (some soils needing more water than others);
— the type of crop (some crops needing more water than others);
— the time of year (some seasons creating a greater demand than others);
— whether the crop has been sown or not;
— whether the water-source is constant or not, which will determine whether only water for immediate use need be taken, or whether some will need to be stored.

Thus any decision as to what is just in a particular situation will be arrived at through consideration of local circumstances.

(C) Artificial canals and irrigation channels. These are treated as joint property. If such channels are filled by tidal action then everyone may take as much as they like because there is enough for everybody. Where this is not the case, such channels belong to those who have dug them and no one else has any right to use them or create further channels leading from them. Furthermore, if someone wants to do something which will affect the level of the water—such as build a pump or a mill that will take up water—this can only be done with the consent of all the others involved, because all concerned have an equal right to the water.

Partially or totally subterranean canal systems, such as the *qanat* system in Iran and the *foggara* system in the Algerian Sahara, also come under the category of rivers, since they are the same as them except that they flow underground.

Once the priority of such rights of usage has been established, the water may then be divided up by time—days if the demand is slight, or hours if the demand is great, and/or by space, for example, by diverting the water into separate channels. It is also possible for each user to fill up a reservoir or use some such other means to store the amount that he needs.

Wells

Wells are also divided into three categories:

(A) Those that have been dug for general public use, in which case everyone has a right to an equal share, with priority being given to people, then livestock, then crops.

(B) Those that have been dug for temporary use, for example a Bedouin encampment, in which case the people who dug them have priority of usage for themselves and their animals, although any excess should be made available to others, based on the hadiths:

> Do not withhold excess water in order to withhold pasture [i.e. prevent it from being grazed].
>
> (Imam Malik, *Muwatta*)

and

> Do not withhold the excess water of a well.
>
> (Imam Malik, *Muwatta*)

When the original users move on, such wells then come under the first category, with priority of usage being on the basis of first come first served, even if the original diggers come back.

(C) Those that have been dug by individuals for their own use. Such wells are considered the property of the person who has dug them, along with the associated harim zone. Once the digging is complete and water has been drawn this person then has total rights to the water and is under no obligation to give any of it away if it is all needed for watering livestock and irrigating crops, except in an emergency such as someone dying of thirst. If there is a surplus left after fulfilling his or her own needs it does not have to be made available for other people's crops but it should be made available for their livestock, provided that:
— the water is still in the well (i.e. that the work of taking it out has not already been done);
— the pasture for the livestock in question is nearby;
— there is no other available and permissible source of water for this livestock;
— no harm accrues to the owner of the well, the owner's livestock or crops as a result of someone else's livestock using the well. Where appropriate, the shepherds may draw the water themselves and take it to their livestock.

Where these conditions are met, in other words where there is reasonable cause to use his water, the owner should make any surplus available without charging for it. A charge may be made for it, however, if any of these conditions are not met.

Springs

This category is also divided into three categories:

(A) Naturally-occurring springs. These come under the same judgement as naturally-occurring rivers, i.e. all are free to use them, on the basis of first come first served, providing either that there is enough water, or, if there is a limited amount of water, that there is an equal division between equally deserving parties.

(B) Springs that have been exploited by individual endeavour on public land. Such a spring, along with its associated harim, is the property of the one who has discovered it. This person may then divert the water wherever he or she likes and the subsequent channels and their associated harims are considered their property.

(C) When someone exploits such a spring on their own property, they then have priority of usage. If there is any surplus, it may be used to reclaim further land and does not have to be made available to other people. If, however, the water is not used in such a way it should be made available for other people's livestock if they need it, but does not have to be made available for their crops (as with wells), and, if it is, a charge can be levied for it.

So we see that the same basic consideration applies to water as applies to land—that there is a distinction between what is public and what is private. In its natural state, water is considered a commonly-held resource, but where someone has dug, say, a well on their private land, they are under no obligation to provide any of the water to anyone else except in cases of emergency.

NATURAL RESOURCES

Natural resources, of which land and water are central, can be divided into what is living and what is not living. What is living sub-divides into animals and plants, while what is not living includes rocks and minerals, thus giving us the three well-known categories of animal, vegetable and mineral.

Animals

Animals can be divided into two main types: domestic and wild. Domestic animals and birds include both those that are kept for food and those that are kept for other purposes. Those kept mainly for food include various kinds of livestock (cattle, sheep and goats etc.) and poultry; while those kept for other purposes include horses, mules and donkeys (for riding and draught), dogs (for guarding and hunting), cats (for ridding the house of mice) etc.

61

Domestic animals

The most important judgements relating to domestic livestock and poultry are:

1 That they are the property of their owners and thus may be bought, sold, given away and inherited.
2 Zakat, or the obligatory annual tax on wealth above a certain minimum, is taken on the basis of those types of livestock that are kept primarily for food, i.e. camels, cattle, sheep and goats, at rates which vary from one type of animal to another (e.g. one sheep for 5–9 camels; one young cow for 30–39 cattle, etc.). No zakat has to be paid on animals that are kept solely for riding and which are not normally eaten, for example, horses.
3 That they should be treated properly, with due respect and without cruelty. The Prophet (S) once said:

> There was once a man walking along a road who became very thirsty. He found a well and so went down into it and drank from it. When he came out he saw a dog which was panting and eating earth because of its thirst, and he said to himself, 'This dog is as thirsty as I was'. So he went down into the well again, filled up his shoe with water, and, holding it in his mouth, came up again and gave it to the dog to drink. Allah thanked him for this and forgave him.

Those listening said:

> O Messenger of Allah, is there a reward for us in animals?

He replied:

> There is a reward in every moist liver [i.e. treating every living animal kindly].
>
> (Imam Malik, *Muwatta*)

In this respect we may also note that the Prophet (S) expressly forbade tying up animals and using them as targets.[1]
4 That when they are killed, they are killed properly and humanely. The Prophet (S) said:

> Allah has prescribed *ihsan* [consideration or excellence] for everything. So when you kill, kill with ihsan; and when you slaughter, slaughter with ihsan. Make sure your knife is sharp, and let your animal die comfortably.
>
> (Muslim)

Animals should be killed efficiently and humanely, and in a way that causes them least anxiety. This is the way that is prescribed by Islamic law, and if an animal is not killed in such a way the meat is considered carrion (*mayta*) and may not be eaten (although it is still permissible to use the hide of such an animal on condition that it has been tanned). One may note here that even when pests are killed, there is a greater reward for killing them with the first blow than with the second.[2]

(See pp. 90–1 for further information on the rights of animals.)

Wild animals

It is permissible to hunt herbivores, for example gazelles, deer, hares, rabbits and non-predatory birds, for food, as long as they are killed correctly. This means either that the hunter himself must kill the game by piercing the body (*'aqr*) with a spear, arrow, bullet, etc. or that the game be killed by a trained animal (dog, cheetah, etc.) or bird (hawk, falcon, etc.). If the hunter can get to the game while it is still alive, without danger, it should be slaughtered in the same way as a domestic animal. It is further permissible to use all parts of animals hunted in such a way. The Haddad in northern Chad, for instance, have traditionally survived on hunting Scimitar-horned oryx, selling the meat and the hides and even using the animals' leg tendons to make nets with which to catch them.[3] It should, however, be pointed out that it is forbidden to hunt any animal which is lawful to eat without having the intention of killing it in the correct manner and for a reasonable purpose. It is also unlawful to hunt an animal with the intention of putting it in a cage, or making a living by it (as with bears and monkeys in circuses, etc.) or even just keeping it as a pet.

Wild carnivores are considered forbidden to eat (or merely disapproved of, according to some authorities), but it is permissible to kill them and other non-edible species if they are a threat or potential threat to either humans, their livestock, crops, or property. Indeed, it is even permissible to kill certain animals in this category (i.e. predators, scavengers and other pests such as wolves, leopards, crows, kites, rats, and scorpions) while on pilgrimage (*hajj*), when any other killing is strictly forbidden. Furthermore, as with animals killed for food, it is permissible to make use of their skins, tusks, sinews, etc. if the animals have been correctly killed, although there is some difference of opinion on this point.

It is forbidden to kill snakes in houses just for the sake of killing them, except for certain kinds known to cause harm. It is, however, permissible to kill snakes in order to eat them as long as one is safe from poison. Lizards may also be killed for food.

All kinds of insects, worms etc. may be killed for food if they are edible, but again, it is forbidden to kill them for no just reason. It is related in the Hadith that one of the previous Prophets once sat down under a tree and was bitten by an ant, whereupon he gave the order for the tree and the ant colony inside it to be burnt. Allah then reproached him, saying,

> Have you destroyed a whole community that glorifies (Me) because of one ant that bit you?
>
> (Muslim)

Plants

Plants can be divided into wild and cultivated. Wild plants, like wild animals, are considered common property, and like wild animals they may be used as food for both humans and livestock and for other purposes such as fuel, fibres, building materials, medicine etc. They can be taken on the basis of first come, first served as long as no harm is done to anyone else.

The specific judgements in Islamic law regarding the cultivation of plants relate primarily to those that are cultivated for food. The important distinction here is between what is storable and what is perishable. Storable foodstuffs include all edible grains, seeds and pulses, and also dried dates, raisins, and oils such as olive oil. Perishable foodstuffs include all kinds of soft fruit and vegetables which are not normally stored. The importance of this distinction is that zakat must be paid on the edible, storable foods mentioned at a rate of one-tenth of every harvest if the land has been watered naturally, or one-twentieth if it has been irrigated. Zakat is not paid on perishables although some authorities say that it should be. Zakat is not taken if the harvest fails to reach a specific minimum (the nisab) of 650 kilos.

There are also specific restrictions on stockpiling basic edibles and on usurious transactions involving any one type of grain etc. This is in addition to the general prohibition of usury with regard to money (see Chapter 5).

It is, therefore, apparent that all living things demand respect and may only be used within very clear limits. It is the nature of existence to be generous. As is well understood by ecologists and others, the vast majority of living organisms reproduce well in excess of the carrying capacity of the ecosystem in which they live, which means there is always potentially plenty to spare. One of Allah's names is the Giver: everything reproduces and produces more. Plants reproduce so that from one grain grows many ears of corn, with many grains in each ear. Our duty is to acknowledge this bounty by giving a portion of crops as zakat. The same applies to domestic animals, which reproduce each year and on which zakat must be paid. Similarly, an individual must also mention the name of the Creator, who gave animals life, when he or she takes their life away. Wild animals are not so freely available as domestic ones, nor are they considered anyone's property (while alive) and, therefore, duties to them are less; the only duty we owe them is that their life should not be taken without reason and if they are killed that this should be done in a correct manner, mentioning the name of the Creator.

It should also be borne in mind that all wild animals and plants are considered common property: all of the above judgements apply so long as no harm is done to anyone else by our use of them, as with water, firewood or pasture. Harm to the creatures of the environment, or to the environment itself, obviously causes harm to the community, and is forbidden on that basis. For example, the destruction of a species with economic value for economic reasons obviously prevents others from being able to benefit from that species, economically or in any other way, and so is forbidden.

Minerals

Mineral deposits come under two categories: 'open' (*zahir*) and 'concealed' (*batin*). 'Open' deposits include deposits of salt, antimony, pitch, etc. which appear on the surface and are easily worked. Such surface deposits are considered common property and may be exploited on the basis of first come, first served, like water. They cannot be assigned by the government (iqta) to particular individuals.

'Concealed' deposits include metals, etc. where work is involved in order to extract the finished product. There are two opinions as to whether they may be assigned to, and exploited by, individuals as their own property. On the basis that they can be assigned, there is a further difference of opinion as to whether such assignation conveys full ownership or merely the right of usufruct during one's life. In other words, such deposits are considered to have been provided naturally without any effort on our part, like game, and therefore there is uncertainty as to whether they can be owned. If, however, someone develops land and then finds a mineral deposit there, he or she is considered the owner and has sole rights in the same way that a person who has created a spring or dug a well has sole rights.

As far as metals are concerned, there is a distinction to be noted between gold and silver, and all other metals. Zakat has to be paid on gold and silver at one-fortieth or 2.5 per cent a year, whereas no zakat has to be paid on any other metal. There are, however, authorities who say that zakat applies to all metals, with some even extending the judgement to include precious stones as well.

Since wealth is one of the 'five essentials' that have to be preserved for society to function smoothly (the other four being religion, life, intellect and family structure), there are numerous judgements that relate to such resources on an economic level e.g. the strictures that relate to all business transactions in general (see Chapter 5). Of these, two judgements stand out over and above all else: namely, the obligation to pay zakat and the prohibition against usury. It is critically important that both of these are put into effect to achieve a just exploitation of natural resources in any Muslim community.

References

1 This ruling is contained in Muslim.
2 This ruling is contained in the *Muwatta* of Imam Malik.
3 See J. Fisher, N. Simon and J. Vincent, *The Red Book: Wildlife in Danger*, Collins, London, 1969, p. 152.

Further note on sources

Many of the details in this chapter were taken from al-Mawardi's *al-Ahkam as-sultaniyya wa-l-wilayat ad-diniyya*, Beirut, 1402/1982, pp. 177–87, 191–4, although extensive recourse was also had to other Arabic sources such as Ibn Rushd's *Bidayat al-mujtahid* and ad-Dasuqi's gloss on ad-Dirdir's *ash-Sharh al-kabir 'ala Mukhtasar Khalil*, especially II:107–108, 115–118, IV:66–75. Other references have been indicated above.

Material on the subject in English is relatively sparse, but the following articles were found to be of particular use (especially the first two for the section 'Himas today'):

J. Grainger and A. Ganadilly, 'Hemas: an investigation into a traditional conservation ethic in Saudi Arabia', *Journal of the Saudi Arabian Natural History Society*, vol. 2, no. 6, July 1986, pp. 28–32.

Harmut Jungius, 'The role of indigenous flora and fauna in rangeland management systems of the arid zones in western Asia', *Journal of Arid Environments*, vol. 6, 1983, pp. 75–85.

Othman Llewellyn, 'Desert reclamation and Islamic law', *The Muslim Scientist*, vol. 11, 1982, pp. 9–29.

J. C. Wilkinson, 'Islamic water law with special reference to oasis settlement', *Journal of Arid Environments*, vol. 1, 1978, pp. 87–96.

بِسْمِ اللَّهِ الرَّحْمَنِ الرَّحِيمِ

5 TRADE AND COMMERCE IN ISLAM

Umar Ibrahim Vadillo and Fazlun M. Khalid

A COMPARISON WITH ECONOMICS

Islamic law defines the boundaries within which trade and business are just. Economics defines the boundaries within which trade and business will be more efficient. Islamic law and economics are two totally different approaches to seeing things which in their turn create two different ways of life. Islam rejects usury (the giving and taking of interest, explained in detail on pp. 71–9) while economics is based on usury. Economics has managed to justify what is Islamically a crime. This is because economics has a method and approach which covers up the inherent injustice of usury. To discuss economics without usury is like expecting a motor car to run without petrol. The one is essential to the other.

In Islam it is necessary to take a different approach altogether to that of economics in order to understand what is just and what is unjust in our commercial behaviour. In the Islamic model what is just is more important than what appears, at first, to be more efficient. Justice is the best guarantee of efficiency. An accepted rule in economics is that if something works efficiently, it is good.

69

This approach, as we will see, hides the true nature of human transactions (the interchange of goods or money) and can have unexpectedly far-reaching effects. Secondly, every transaction, as a unit, should be just in order for trade to be just. While economics looks at trade as something to be encouraged in its totality, it has by comparison ignored its most basic element which is the transaction itself. In Islamic law justice should be applied in the transaction. An example of this kind of transaction would be the exchange of a carpet for five sacks of wheat or an agreed amount of gold. The value of the gold and the wheat has been determined by the parties who are making the transaction. The introduction of paper money would distort the transaction because its value is determined by remote external forces, such as interest rates and exchange controls, that are not related to that transaction.

Transactions are the basic first steps to trade. Understanding this will help us appreciate why matters can go very wrong if certain principles are not followed. It can be compared to erecting a building on unstable foundations: the building may look strong but will eventually collapse. The same rule applies in trade. The foundations of trade are rooted in the transaction and sound trans-actions will guarantee sound trade.

The foundations for all human transactions were laid down in the Qur'an over 1,400 years ago. These foundations are for all time and Islamic law is based on this. Societies may change but the basic nature of transactions between people does not. The study of economics is a recent invention (approximately 200 years old). It is described as a science by many, but it is not. For example, there can be many, often conflicting ways of interpreting a given econ-omic situation, depending on the politics and ideology of the writer.

We can conclude from this that there is no such thing as Islamic economics because the basis of economics is not merely outside the scope of Islamic principles, it is opposed to it.

RENTABLE AND NON-RENTABLE MERCHANDISE

Before we examine usury itself it will be useful to have a brief discussion on the nature of things which are bought and sold. There are two types of merchandise, the first can be rented for specific periods of time and then returned, for example: houses, cars, horses or machines. The second type cannot be rented, it is bought and consumed, for example: food, gas or oil.

What about money itself? Is it rentable or non-rentable? It is only useful when it can be spent although it remains in existence after it has been spent. (This will become clearer when the nature of money is understood. This is explained in the section entitled 'Imposed medium of exchange'.) As far as the spender is concerned the money has been consumed as though it were an apple. Therefore, money is non-rentable. This is why from the earliest beginnings of human history renting money was considered to be cheating. Having established that money by itself is not productive or rentable, we are now better placed to study usury.

The Prophet of Islam (S) said:

> A dinar for a dinar, a dirham for a dirham, no excess between the two.
>
> (Imam Malik, *Muwatta*)

WHAT IS USURY?

Allah says in the Qur'an:

> That they used usury though it was forbidden and that they usurped men's wealth with falsehood.
>
> (Qur'an 2:161)

In this verse Allah speaks about a people who resorted to certain practices involving usury. It is clear from this verse that usury, taking what belongs to others, is forbidden in Islam.

In another Qur'anic verse Allah says:

> Allah has allowed trade, but has forbidden usury.
>
> (Qur'an 2:275)

71

Usury has been condemned by many important men in history. Plato, the Greek philosopher, considered usury to be the enemy of social well-being because it created a class of rich lenders at the expense of the impoverished borrowers. The Roman writers Seneca and Cicero compared it to murder; the Christian saints Augustine and Thomas Aquinas compared the usurer to someone who tries to sell wine and its use separately.

It is said in the defence of usury that it is the same as trade, but it is actually the opposite. True trade is based on justice, that is the exchange of equal for equal. Usurious trade is based on injustice, that is asking something more and giving something less or nothing in return. According to Qadi Abu Bakr, a twelfth-century CE Muslim teacher, usury is 'any unjust increment between the value of the goods given and the value of the goods received'. The opposite of this is the just transaction. A just commercial transaction is an agreement for the exchange of goods established with equity and acceptance by both parties. Equity means that a value is put on the goods when they are being exchanged and that this is done in a market that is not restricted. It also means that those who are involved in this exchange agree that the conditions are fair and open. Equity guarantees that equal amounts of goods or money have been exchanged. If restrictions are placed on the market then there cannot be an equal exchange of goods. For example, if the price of apples is raised by all the farmers who grow them, then as the sellers they have an unfair advantage over the buyers. There are other conditions to an exchange of goods which make a transaction false and unequal. This can happen when a price is quoted for the weight or volume of a thing whose value is unknown and can also happen when interest is charged when money is lent. Charging interest is like asking for rent on cash and it distorts the balance of a transaction since it artificially distorts the price before an exchange has taken place. An equitable transaction is equal for equal. Usury is something for nothing.

The profit of trade is not usury since at least two transactions are needed to make a profit. Profits are not made in a single transaction because the goods in the transaction are equivalent. Profits are made or losses suffered when the difference between two transactions is compared. This difference occurs when something is bought for a certain price and then transported or transformed or processed and sold for a different price. This is the legal profit of trade. But the profit of usury takes place when there is only one transaction. In this exchange a condition is introduced by which one party to the transaction will receive more than is put in by the second party. A profit is made in a single transaction by doing nothing. One example of this kind of transaction is the lottery. The conditions of a lottery are always usurious regardless of the winners or losers. A winner receives more than the price of a lottery ticket and the loser receives nothing.

The profit of usury is like a parasite in a market—it sucks in wealth without giving anything in return. The parasite forces the market to increase artificially in size, like a diseased body, just so it can feed. But as the market grows, the parasite also grows. Usury produces an imbalance in natural trading, and this has now penetrated everything. In order to understand how usury distorts transactions we will take a closer look at the basics of trade.

DIFFERENT FORMS OF USURY

Allah says in the Qur'an:

> O my people! give full measure and full weight with equity, and wrong not people in respect of their things, and act not corruptly in the land making mischief.
>
> (Qur'an 11:85)

Usury has been defined as asking something for nothing in a single transaction. It is the opposite of a just or equivalent transaction. It is not equal for equal. The natural equity of a transaction is altered when usury is introduced. There are two basic ways of altering the equity of a transaction:

(a) By controlling the market and therefore destroying the freedom of the market.
(b) By imposing a condition in a transaction that is unrelated to that particular transaction and therefore destroying the equal balance of the values of the goods in the transaction.

73

Control of the market

The first form of usury is called *riba al-fadl* in Arabic and consists of tampering with the freedom of the market thus affecting all the transactions of that market. This can be further sub-divided into five different types.

1 Monopoly and monopsony

Monopoly is controlling the production or distribution of any marketable thing. Monopsony is controlling the buying of a thing in a market. They are both devices by which a sufficient quantity of a particular thing is disposed of or acquired by an individual or group to prevent the free pricing of that thing taking place in a market.

The second Caliph of Islam, 'Umar ibn al-Khattab, said:

> There is no hoarding in our market and men who have excess gold in their hands should not buy up one of Allah's provisions which he has sent to our courtyard and then hoard it up against us . . .
>
> (Imam Malik, *Muwatta*)

2 Price control

This happens when the state or a powerful group imposes minimum, maximum or fixed prices for a thing. For example, socialist countries control prices as part of their political control.

3 Taxation

Free access to markets can also be controlled by taxing trade. Any tax on trading restricts trade itself and this method is usually used to control the free market in capitalist countries. The only tax in Islam is known as zakat. This is not a tax on trading or on income. It is also not a state tax. It is collected by the community and immediately distributed to groups in need including the poor, the sick and those who have no home. Taxation and any other form of state control on trading does not exist in Islam.

4 Imposed medium of exchange

The most widely used medium of exchange in everyday transactions throughout the world today is paper money. We are led to believe that this money is worth more than the paper it is printed on, but it is the law that we use it for exchange. This is not permitted in Islamic law as it comes within the definition of usury, imposed by the state. In the Islamic market people are free to choose their medium of exchange to suit their own circumstances and every market is free to decide what this medium will be by common consent. Therefore, money in an Islamic market is defined as 'any merchandise commonly accepted as a medium of exchange'.

Before the state, with the assistance of the banks, imposed the use of paper money, gold and silver were universally accepted as mediums of exchange, with local markets freely choosing different commodities like salt, leather or copper as mediums of exchange. The price of gold, silver and the other mediums of exchange fluctuated because they were allowed to circulate freely in the market. In an Islamic market the flexibility of the medium of exchange is maintained and is not imposed, and the value of a thing is determined exclusively by the people transacting in any given market.

Today the use of paper money is imposed and it has been made unlawful to use any other parallel currency. However, the banks, with the aid of the state, are able to invent other means of exchange like charge cards and credit cards, thus bypassing the use of paper money. But the principle behind these means of exchange remains the same: to transfer a notion of value with something which in itself has no value. This ostensibly works because it is assumed that this paper or card transaction has a guaranteed fixed value, but this is only true for the very short term. It is no secret that money undergoes a continuous and permanent reduction in its value. This reduction in what money can buy is called inflation. To make up what is called 'purchasing power' people borrow from the banks. The banks can create credit. This means they can create money. They do this by legally lending anything between ten and twenty times more than what they hold as cash. This unreal money then competes with itself and real money, for the purchase of things which are scarce and which become scarcer because they are being chased by more and more money. This causes further inflation and a further drop in the value of the money that people have in their hands. This is a usurious crime in Islam.

5 Exclusive rights of authors and inventors

There is a right in law which guarantees a monopoly, through copyright and rights of patent, for authors and inventors for their lifetime. These rights were first legalized 130 years ago in France. They did not exist previously. They are based on the notion that a person can claim ownership of an idea or concept. Muslims know that all knowledge belongs to Allah. He is the source of everything and what we know comes from Him. An idea is always based on something. It is the aggregation of other ideas and knowledge left by other people. There is no justice in a situation where a person can claim exclusive rights to an idea but is not expected to compensate others on whose ideas theirs is based.

In practice the rights of patent restrict the access of industrial products to the market through artificially raising the price, because the supply is controlled. It is not dissimilar to an absolute monopoly. In international trade relations this is tantamount to a burden imposed by industrial countries on developing countries. The rights of patent have also obstructed the process by which knowledge is freely shared and have restricted all fields of endeavour for the purpose of protecting copyrights and patents.

Controlling the market by any means is usurious and five such methods have been discussed above. The main principle in an Islamic transaction is the freedom of that transaction. Any device that impedes justice or equality in a transaction and which artificially reduces or increases the price of a thing is a crime in Islamic law.

Inequality in transactions

The second form of usury is called *riba al-nasiah* in Arabic. It consists of the establishment of conditions within a contract of exchange which are unequal, that is, which create a situation where one party to a contract has a built-in advantage over the other. There are three main types of transaction that come within this category.

1 The renting of money

Renting money is the most condemned form of usury. Money can be sold (exchanged) and can be invested in a business. But it cannot be rented. A guaranteed fixed return on an investment regardless of the outcome of that investment is forbidden. Islamic law requires that the investor shares both in the success and the failure of a venture depending on the mutually agreed contract. Anything other than this is tantamount to renting money, and as we have seen earlier, money cannot be rented like a house because it is a non-rentable commodity. A profit from money can only be justified if it is invested in a business and that business produces a profit. Money by itself cannot produce a profit.

The institutions best known for making money out of money are the banks. The monies they use to do this are the deposits made by other people. That is, money that does not belong to the banks. Additionally, every commercial bank can lend ten to twenty times (depending on the laws of the country concerned) more than they have in deposits. This, legal, banking device enables banks to create money. To protect themselves the banks function as a consortium which guarantees that the system works. Together they cover the demand for cash which they cope with through a system called 'clearing'. It will be seen that the banks lend money although they hold only a small proportion of it in cash. Borrowers rent, that is pay interest, on this imaginary money which the banks have legally created. This is *riba* (usury) within Islamic law, and it is not permitted.

The banks' activities have altered the nature of money. Through their ability to create artificial money the banks have created artificial wealth. That is, something out of nothing. It is also a fact that this artificial money can in turn be made into bank deposits which can again be used by the banks to lend in multiples of ten to twenty. This explosion of artificial wealth which remains in the hands of a small minority has been used to exploit the real wealth of people which is finite and limited. The effects of this have been devastating globally through the emergence of powerful nations and giant companies which destroy traditional lifestyles and livelihoods and which irreversibly damage the environment. All this and much more are the effects stemming from the practice of usury.

2 Uncertainty in transactions

For any transaction to be the exchange of equal for equal, the quality, quantity and price of the merchandise being exchanged have to be clearly defined. Uncertainty in a transaction produces an imbalance in the value of the goods in exchange and is therefore usurious. As stated earlier, a lottery, dealing in unknown quantities, the futures market (buying wheat, coffee, sugar etc. before the crops are harvested) are all classified as usurious. Buying shares in limited liability companies is usurious for two reasons. Firstly because liability is limited. This means that shareholders are protected from having to pay creditors should the business collapse. Secondly, because shareholders have a very limited involvement in the running of the business as is apparent in their remoteness from the decision-making centre of a company.

3 Unfair advantages in transactions

Any transactions that in any way hide or distort the eventual price of a thing fall into this category. Examples of these are: bidding at an auction with the sole intention of raising the price without the intention of buying; agreeing to a loan on the condition that the price of an unrelated thing that the lender desires will be reduced in price; raising the price of a thing to take advantage of a temporary visitor such as a tourist or pilgrim.

It will be seen from what we have been discussing that usury is any transaction by which one party to it benefits without giving fair and reasonable return to the other. The Islamic market guarantees that there is no usury by insisting on openness and equality on every transaction and that gain is related to the freely negotiated price in free market conditions. To make a gain or profit there need to be at least two transactions or exchanges, the difference between the two being the profit. The introduction of usurious exchange into a market creates imbalance and distortions because the usurers benefit without putting anything into the transaction. Their main objective is to benefit from other people's transactions without being involved in the risk of a project or the problems of the market. They function like parasites and destroy the health of a transaction and subsequently entire markets. This is why usury is regarded as a crime in Islam.

OWNERSHIP AND ITS IMPLICATIONS

The growth of banking in the seventeenth century CE created an explosion of credit which has been increasing ever since. People sought outlets for the money they possessed and this quite frequently took the form of purchasing shares in trading companies known as joint stock companies. The shares were split into small marketable units for convenience. Furthermore the concept of limited liability was introduced about the mid-nineteenth century CE and this caused a further boost in the trading of shares. As we have seen shareholders in a limited liability company have the unique advantage of being liable for losses only to the extent of the value of their shares. Again, uniquely, limited liability companies are recognized in law as being persons in their own right. These companies are based on principles of ownership which are unacceptable in Islam: that is, limited risk and remoteness from decision-making centres. An important factor arising out of this is that it is now possible for an individual or small group of people to control a business at the expense of the rest through a device known as 'majority ownership'.

Ownership in a free and natural system gives the owner two main rights in a business or property. The first is the freedom to dispose of that business as and when he chooses, and the second is to participate in the decision-making process of that business. Therefore, the essence of ownership can be defined as the right of an owner to make decisions about his business or property without artificial impediments.

The essence of ownership

Ownership gives the owner of something the right to use or consume that thing. That right is earned by virtue of the owner of that thing acquiring it through honest endeavour or through an exchange in a just transaction. Natural resources are Allah's gift to mankind and there are no restrictions on their use provided that what is taken is to satisfy need and not to gratify greed. Sometimes, however, artificial controls have to be imposed on the exploitation of certain resources, as they could become scarce for various reasons such as natural causes or overuse. One such example is fishing. As populations grow and fishing fleets increase fish become scarce. In this situation a community is at liberty to conserve stocks by regulating catches.

The space above the ground, the space we call the atmosphere is free. It belongs to everyone and it would be ridiculous to have to pay for it. But the fact is we have to pay for its use through taxes. An obvious example of this is tall buildings, where floors above ground level are also taxed; another example is TV and radio frequencies, where airwaves are reserved for named transmitters who are then taxed.

However, we establish ownership of the space around us by being in it and breathing the air it contains. Similarly aircraft claim ownership of a flight path by being in it and using it. Nobody else can occupy a space occupied by another person and no other thing can be in a space already occupied. This obvious fact establishes the principle that ownership exists every time something is used, and the user is the owner.

Explicitly regulated or not, ownership is intrinsically connected to the use of things. Ownership cannot be done away with as long as things are made use of. The use of things implies that a decision has been made about its use. Whoever made that decision effectively owned whatever was consumed or made use of. This person, by exercising the rights of ownership, is the actual owner of that thing—the entitled owner. This type of ownership is preserved in Islamic law.

In the light of this statement it is possible to say something very important. Privacy is the essence of ownership because, as we have seen in the discussion above, decisions to use or consume something ultimately remain private. Furthermore, this decision-making process can be either individual or collective. When ownership is exercised individually there is no difficulty in understanding how decisions are made. But what happens when there is collective ownership? How does a group exercise their collective rights of ownership? In Islamic law the co-owners submit to two principles. They are:

1 All the co-owners have equal decision-making powers regardless of the amount they have invested. If this condition is not fulfilled then one party is seen to have an advantage over the others, who cease to be the effective owners.
2 The results of the venture are shared amongst the co-owners in proportion to their investment.

Islamic law requires a contract to be written every time there is a commercial agreement between two or more persons. This contract is what constitutes the private decisions of the business. The business contract clearly defines in advance the nature of the business. It identifies the investors, the agent (if there is one), the amounts invested, and states the aims of the business. It also specifies the duration of the venture and how profit will be shared. When a contract of this nature is signed all the parties to it know from the outset exactly what is involved and no one has any advantages over the others. This is the opposite of what we are familiar with today. It is customary now for an investor to put his money in a venture of no fixed duration where those who decide how the profits are shared are not the owners. This situation goes against natural organic trading and is outside the framework of Islamic practice. A description of how this came about follows.

Distorted ownership

One of the major financial institutions in the world today is the stock exchange, also known as the stock market. These markets began their careers in the late eighteenth century and continued to grow vigorously as a result of the factors we have discussed: the

explosion of credit through the growth of banking and the introduction of the concept of limited liability. We have also seen that
majority ownership became a legal possibility because of these
developments. The stock markets have played a major role in
distorting ownership. Majority ownership of companies provided
the opportunity for individuals and small groups to take what is
known as a controlling interest in a company. All large companies, particularly multi-nationals, are run like this today. This
situation is usually brought about by taking control of the majority of the available shares in a company. This leaves the other
shareholders in a position which is contractually unacceptable in
Islamic law. Although they may be part-owners of a business by
contract, they do not have effective decision-making powers even
over their share in the business.

This system of majority or controlling ownership allows the
control of significant portions of a particular market by one individual or small group of people. The following example shows
how majority ownership can usurp the rights of millions of
minority co-owners:

> Mr Stone owns 51 per cent of Company A and, therefore, has
> control of that company and the power to dispose of its capi-
> tal. If he uses capital from Company A to buy 51 per cent of
> Company B he will have total control of Company B
> although he personally owns approximately one quarter of its
> capital. If he then uses the capital of Company B to buy 51 per
> cent of Company C he will have total control of C although
> he personally owns only one eighth of the capital. Mr Stone
> can then go on to buy Companies D, E, and F in the same
> way. (In reality people who own much less than a half-share
> of a company may actually control it through a device known
> as the 'controlling interest'.)

Thus we see how Mr Stone, who is now strictly a minority
shareholder himself, has power over an enormous amount of capital that is obviously not his. He is able to decide the proportion of
the profits to be distributed in the form of dividends to other
shareholders and he is now in a position where through the chain
of ownership he can take control of all the companies.

The profits of a business do not end with the dividends. The assets or capital of a successful business also increase in value and the only way to discover the real value of a business at the end of a given period is to liquidate it. That is turn it into cash. But the device of majority or controlling ownership prevents this happening, thus putting the minority shareholders at a disadvantage. The entire decision-making process is controlled by the majority shareholder who, as we have seen, may well not actually own the majority of a business. The minority shareholders dissatisfied with the way a company is run can do only two things: either protest at the annual general meeting of shareholders, or sell their shares on the stock market. The usual option is to sell their shares. Normal stock market prices do not reflect the total value of a company. This only comes to light when predatory bids leading to what are popularly known as 'takeover battles' are made by majority owners of other companies.

Allah says in the Qur'an:

> O you who believe, devour not your property among yourself by illegal methods, but let there be among you trading by mutual consent . . .
>
> (Qur'an 4:29)

THE ISLAMIC MODEL

Trade in Islam is free of the constraints and complications that keep people away from transacting with each other freely and openly. We have seen earlier that trade is allowed and that usury (riba) is forbidden, and we have examined the different forms of it. What we need to understand is that the term usury only partly explains riba which is far more comprehensive and all-embracing in its application.

The central position in Islam on riba and trade is further emphasized in three verses in the Qur'an:

> O you who believe
> Fear Allah and give up
> What remains of your demand

83

For usury, if you are
Indeed believers.

If you do it not
Take notice of war
From Allah and his messenger:
But if you turn back
You shall have your capital sums;
Deal not unjustly
And you shall not be dealt with unjustly.

If the debtor is in a difficulty,
Grant him time till it is easy for him to repay
But if ye remit it by way of charity
That is best for you if ye only knew.

(Qur'an 2:278, 279, 280)

To trade in the Islamic way is to bypass the banks and go back to the community where people who trade know each other or use the medium of a business agent who is a trusted, knowledgeable member of the community. The agent, unlike a bank, brings entrepreneurs together in transactions without riba.

Many Islamic community-based transactions exist today, particularly in areas remote from the banks. There is also a growing movement to establish Islamic markets in urban and metropolitan areas. There are three stages to this development, which is known as the *Qirad* system of trading.

Stage 1—Trading without bank finance but with paper money.

Stage 2—Trading without banks and paper money. The introduction of bartering.

Stage 3—Trading with bartering and a fluid currency system. No taxation on trading (possible only in Muslim countries where Islamic law applies). The rules in Islam encourage people to trade in a natural organic way within the resources that are made available to them by the Creator. Riba is an all-embracing concept and is forbidden. This, until recent times, has prevented the formation of a small class of powerful people in whose hands wealth is concentrated as a result of their ability to control the banks and the big trading institutions. As we have seen banks are able to create wealth out of nothing. This 'non-wealth' is then used to exploit the real wealth of the world. The destruction of our environment must be seen in this light.

We know that the paper money which we use in our transactions every day is only a token and not worth anything. We do not question its use because it has been made and it has become essential to our lives. It has been forced on us. We are so familiar with it that we do not question how we use it or question the basic assumptions that lie behind its very existence. Some say that this whole business of banks and money is like a new religion that we all practice without being aware that we subscribe to it. The Islamic model points to a system where neither banks nor paper money prevail. That is a return to the natural state. A state of balance where transactions are conducted on the basis of a true and observed value of things.

Note

Material for this chapter in addition to the Qur'an has been drawn from the *Muwatta* of Imam Malik.

بِسْمِ اللَّهِ الرَّحْمَنِ الرَّحِيمِ

6 DESERT RECLAMATION AND CONSERVATION IN ISLAMIC LAW

Othman Llewellyn

Most of the arid lands of Africa and Asia fall within the regions where Islam is the major religion. Reclaiming the desert lands and using them for agriculture, grazing or building is becoming ever more important as populations grow and the need for food increases. Presently, however, these lands are badly mismanaged and are rapidly deteriorating.

Making life flourish in the land (*ihya al-mawat*) has always been an important value in Islam. The long experience of Muslim scholars who have made decisions on the use and management of scarce resources is of immense value in the planning of desert reclamation.

The aims of Shari'ah, Islamic law, are directly relevant for desert reclamation. The ultimate goal is that all created beings will benefit through wise and just use of natural resources. The most efficient ways of using the land, without abusing it, should be found, and starvation amongst livestock should be eliminated. Islamic law contains important principles and precepts which govern the use of property, water rights, maintenance of livestock, hunting, and public access to resources that are needed for survival.

Arid lands are generally the last type of land to undergo development but demands on fertile land have been so great and its resources so overused that the time is coming when arid lands will have to be developed to provide grazing for livestock and to sustain crops that can flourish around the oases. They will have to provide minerals for industries and their inhabitants will require adequate shelter and transport. These lands must also serve as the last refuge of many forms of wildlife.

How can these lands best be reclaimed within the limitations of scarce water supply, poor soil, harsh climate and a fragile balance of animal and plant life which could easily be destroyed if the land is exploited by human settlement? The solutions will demand the finest skills of land, water, wildlife, crop and soil management and of planning and design.

The farmers and nomads of these lands are mostly poor with little or no formal education. Their settlements are widely scattered and solutions to the problems cannot involve expensive outlay or the widespread use of modern technology. The arid lands are thinly populated and therefore projects to reclaim the land have to use a small labour force. It is low-cost, small-scale, long-lasting and easily maintained solutions that are needed. The way ahead must appeal to the strongly held Muslim values of the people and must turn to the areas of Islamic law that may have been discarded. No believing Muslim can make any design or plan, except in accordance with the will of Allah. Making life flourish in the land has always been an important value in Islam and it is in the wisdom of the Shari'ah that solutions may be found.

THE OBJECTIVES OF THE SHARI'AH

The Shari'ah must be understood in the light of the Islamic teaching regarding the purpose of law and the purpose of human existence. The purpose of the Shari'ah flows from the belief that there is but one God, Lord of all beings on whom all created beings depend. He has designed creation and creatures are made to be dependent on each other so that each group works for the welfare of the other. Ultimately, life and death are created by Allah so that living beings may serve Him by good works:

> Blessed is He in whose hand is dominion, and He has power over everything—He who has created life and death to try you, which of you do work the most good.
>
> (Qur'an 67:2)

On the basis of Allah's guidance in the Qur'an, Muslim legal scholars have defined the ultimate objective of the Shari'ah as the universal common good of all created beings, both in this life and in the life after death. Working for the good of all creation is the only way that one can truly serve Allah.

The following sayings of the Prophet Muhammad (S) express the profound religious and ethical value of bringing new life to the land:

> Whoever brings dead land to life, for him is a reward in it, and whatever any creature seeking food eats of it shall be reckoned as charity from him.
>
> (*Mishkat al-Masabih*)

> There is no Muslim who plants a tree or sows a field, and a human, bird or animal eats from it, but it shall be reckoned as charity from him.
>
> (*Mishkat al-Masabih*)

It is recorded that the Prophet Muhammad (S) prohibited the cutting of any tree in the desert which provided valuable shade or sustenance either for humans or animals, and that he established protected zones around Makkah, al Madinah and al Ta'if, within which he forbade the cutting of native trees and the hunting of wildlife.

The attitude of the Shari'ah towards the use and development of the earth's resources was accurately summed up by the Prophet's (S) follower and cousin, 'Ali ibn Abi-Talib, who said to a man who had dug canals and reclaimed abandoned land:

> Partake of it with joy, so long as you are a benefactor, not a corruptor, a cultivator, not a destroyer.
>
> (Yahya ibn Adam)

89

LEGAL PRINCIPLES

Many of the specific rulings of the Shari'ah were organized by Muslim legal scholars into general principles (*Qawa'id*) which are useful in understanding the Islamic approach to legal problems, including issues related to desert reclamation. The principles which relate to the use of property are particularly relevant.

Although the right to hold private property is fundamental in Islamic law, Islamic teaching maintains that Allah is the one real owner of the earth and all that it contains. All property and resources are given in trust to human beings to be used only in accordance with divine purposes. Therefore, the right to hold private property is safeguarded but there are important restrictions on its use.

Amongst the most basic principles of Islamic law is the declaration of the Prophet Muhammad (S) that

> There shall be no injury and no perpetration of injury.
>
> (Yahya ibn Adam)

Muslim legal scholars have understood this to mean that no one should cause undue injury to another created thing nor should they abuse the basic rights that they have been given. This guidance is particularly relevant when it comes to the use of resources such as water, pasture, woodlands, wildlife, and certain minerals. These are entrusted to public management so that all people can have equal access to their benefits.

Following this guidance, a farm beside a stream is forbidden to claim all rights over its water. After using or storing a certain amount of water for his crops, the farmer must release the rest to those downstream. Furthermore, if there is not enough water for all the farms along the stream the older farms are to be satisfied before the newer farms are permitted to irrigate. This system allows a limited number of farms in the watershed to flourish, rather than encouraging unlimited farms who would put too many demands on the water supply, so that in the end everyone would suffer.

Undue injury to animals was also prohibited by the Prophet Muhammad (S). It is a distinctive characteristic of Islamic law that all animals have legal rights. The thirteenth-century CE legal scholar 'Izz ad-Din ibn 'Abd as-Salam formulated the following statement of rights based on stories and sayings of the Prophet (S):

> The rights of livestock and animals upon man:
>
> These are that he spend on them the provision that their kinds require, even if they have aged or sickened such that no benefit comes from them; that he not burden them beyond what they can bear; that he not put them together with anything by which they would be injured, whether of their own kind or other species, whether by breaking their bones or butting or wounding; that he slaughter them with kindness; that when he slaughters them he neither flay their skins nor break their bones until their bodies have become cold and their lives have passed away; that he not slaughter their young within their sight but that he isolate them; that he make comfortable their resting places and watering places; that he put their males and females together during their mating seasons; that he not discard those which he takes as game; and neither shoot them with anything that breaks their bones nor bring about their destruction by any means that renders their meat unlawful to eat.
>
> (Ibn Abd As-Salam)

Many Muslim legal scholars have declared that the rights of animals must be enforced by the state. When these rights are put into practice they are bound to have a strong influence on farming and ranching practice.

Corruption of the earth (*al-fasad fi 'lard*) such as the destruction of crops, livestock and the environment in general is forbidden in the Qur'an. Unnecessary waste is also forbidden in times of plenty as well as in times of drought or famine. The Prophet (S) forbade a person to waste water even in washing for prayer on the bank of an abundantly flowing river.

To avoid corruption, destruction and waste, methods of desert reclamation should be used that conserve as many natural resources as possible and cause the minimum amount of environmental damage. These methods should include appropriate siting, planning, building and use of materials that make use of the wind, sun and available rain. To minimize the waste of life careful methods of pest control should be employed and gardens should be at once supremely beautiful and supremely useful, to make best use of water and arable land.

91

Among the most important principles in Islamic law are those which enable a person or group to make a fair judgement when the interests of several groups come into conflict. A decision should be made that takes into account the good or harm that will result from a certain action. If an action causes as much good as it does damage, then that action will be forbidden, or if a decision must be made between the needs of the poor and the needs of the rich the poor must be given preference. The wider interests of society and of creation as a whole take priority over the narrower interests of individuals and particular groups. Absolute necessities such as religion, morality, life, children, family, reason, mental health and property have the highest priority; lesser needs follow and the last considerations are luxuries, refinements and perfections. The following principles of Islamic law show how these priorities can be put into practice.

INSTITUTIONS OF ISLAMIC LAW

Several institutions or areas of Islamic law are of vital yet little recognized importance to the problems of agriculture, forest and wildlife management and town planning which involves reclaiming desert lands. These areas of the law include:

(a) *ihya*, acquiring unowned land through reclamation (bringing life to the land);
(b) *iqta*, land granted by the state to cultivators;
(c) *ijarah*, leasing land to cultivators;
(d) *harim*, protected zones;
(e) *hima*, reserves of land established for public purposes and for preservation of natural habitat;
(f) *waqf*, land given charitably for the public good;
(g) *hisbah*, the office of public inspector to ensure public and private land, resources and property are used correctly.

Ihya

Lands that are uncultivated or abandoned and belong to nobody may be acquired by anyone who 'brings them to life' in the language of Islamic law. This principle was established by the Prophet Muhammad (S), in his declaration that

> Whoever revives dead land, it shall be his.
>
> (Bukhari)

A cultivator may stake a claim to vacant land by fencing it in and then reclaiming it through planting, building, draining, digging a well or irrigating. Grazing the land alone does not mean that it has been brought back to life. If the land has not been revived after a reasonable length of time, usually three years, the cultivator loses his rights of ownership and others have a right to reclaim it.

Acquiring land through ihya is permitted as long as this does not harm the general welfare of the community and the environment. For example, a cultivator cannot claim watercourses, roads, public squares, the pastures or woodlands belonging to villagers or wildlife habitats.

Iqta

The state may grant areas of unowned or state-owned land to cultivators who accept the responsibility of reclaiming the land. The efforts of their work on this land must, however, benefit themselves and the community. Until the cultivator can prove that the land has been revived and put to good use he cannot be granted ownership of that land. If the land has not been revived within three years others may have the opportunity of reviving it. The state may not grant more land than any person is capable of reclaiming since this not only places pressure on the owner but also denies rights of land to others. Iqta may only be granted if the land does not contain sources of surface water, valuable minerals, or other resources upon which the public good depends.

Land grants are usually areas of land that cannot be reclaimed through the normal process of ihya because of their remoteness or difficulty of access. These grants could be awarded competitively to individuals or companies submitting the most suitable plans and designs for reclamation.

Ijarah

Lands may be leased by their owners to cultivators to grow specified crops or make specified improvements. The lease of state-owned land is particularly relevant in this aspect of Islamic law. Before an agreement is reached the rental fee, the period of use and the uses must all be clearly specified. If the land is put to any use not mentioned in the contract this must not cause more damage than would have occurred had the contract been strictly adhered to.

During the period of the contract the person who has leased the land has ownership over improvements such as trees or buildings and when the lease expires, unless the contract says otherwise, he or she has the right to buy them, renew the lease or remove them at their own expense. If the person who has signed the lease dies before it ends then it is inherited by his or her heirs.

The exploitation of tenant farmers was forbidden by the Prophet Muhammad (S). He encouraged farmers to loan unused lands to others without charge. It is therefore important that the state charges a minimum fee for such leases, a fee that the poorest farmer can afford.

When land is leased the state retains the right to supervise its use and if the land is needed for public use it can be taken back at any time. Historically, the long-term lease of state land has been used to develop new settlements, expand watercourses and revitalize decayed or abandoned areas. Today, ecologically sensitive lands such as those which have been eroded by deforestation, overgrazing or overcultivation, or those which contain valuable resources can be taken over by the state and managed for the benefit of the public. These sensitive lands should be taken over, even from private ownership, and just compensation offered. If some of these lands could be improved through certain types of agriculture then the state should lease them to cultivators, as long as the public would benefit from their use. The state would, however, retain control of the use of the land and could stipulate which crops should be grown and how the land should be managed. Leases could be awarded to those who submit the most appropriate plans or designs and should be sufficiently long-term to be worth the farmer's effort and investment.

The harim and hima

In Islamic law there are zones, known as harim, around watercourses, wells, crops and settlements. Development is restricted or prohibited in these areas to prevent damage to important resources. Harim can be individually owned: for example, the land around a private well, or they can be publicly owned: for example, the undeveloped land around a town or village which provides forage and firewood for the community and a safe habitat for wildlife. The banks of natural watercourses and the land bordering roads are usually managed by the state.

In Islamic law there are also areas of land that are declared to be reserves so that they can be protected for the public good; these are known as hima. A hima can be a reserve for forest conservation or for wildlife and hunting; grazing and woodcutting are usually prohibited within its boundaries. Some hima permit seasonal grazing and during periods of drought communities may receive permission to graze a limited number of animals for a certain period. Trespassers on these lands are fined and jailed.

Hima and harim share a similar purpose but harim are managed by individuals or the community and are found around settlements; hima can be found anywhere and are managed by the state for the benefit of the public and other created beings.

(For a more detailed account of harim and hima see Chapter 4, pp. 53–6.)

Waqf

The waqf or charitable endowment is the aspect of Islamic law which allows a person to dedicate property for the benefit of the public. Waqf properties are dedicated to Allah for all time and should be used for a specified beneficial purpose. This charitable gift becomes public property that cannot be given away, sold, mortgaged, inherited or otherwise disposed of, but it may take the form of a land trust. The waqf is administered according to the wishes of the person who donated it and its administration is carried out by the qadi, the local magistrate. The waqf can only run efficiently if it is administered wisely.

Any public work such as a garden or orchard, well, mosque, hospital, school or college may be run for all time as a waqf. The income of a farm or business that is run through a waqf may be reserved for charitable purposes. Through these charitable endowments, a vast pool of public buildings and land accumulates over the years. In the Sahara, the religious brotherhoods of the Sanusiyah and Shaykhiyah reclaimed extensive areas of desert by establishing them as waqf lands used for the common good.

The waqf should be encouraged to give individuals or small groups the chance to take part in long-term reclamation projects that will benefit the community and the environment. As trusts or endowments they could establish agricultural research stations and experimental farms, training institutes, wildlife breeding farms and habitat development. The most essential element of a successful waqf is efficient management. Standards should be set for the management of these endowments and for the qualifications of their managers so that they can achieve their full potential.

Hisbah

Hisbah is the office of public inspection which is traditional in Islamic law. While every adult Muslim is charged with the duty to establish good and eradicate evil, this office was established by the Islamic state to ensure that this was carried out. This office was headed by the muhtasib who worked under the qadi and was charged with the inspection of markets, buildings, streets and so forth. He was responsible for the enforcement of standards, the removal of nuisances and hazards, the elimination of corrupt and unethical business practices, and the prevention of animal abuse. This role has almost disappeared but its revival in the community would work towards Islamic principles being established in social transactions so that some would not take advantage of others or make unjust profits.

If the office of hisbah was applied to desert reclamation it would be responsible for the inspection of all constructions of buildings, dams, irrigation systems, and livestock enclosures. It should be responsible for the supervision of harim zones and hima reserves, the enforcement of hunting regulations, and the prevention of overgrazing and destructive farming practices. Likewise, it should be responsible for the inspection of livestock and enforcement of their proper maintenance, the supervision of their slaughter and the inspection of meat and of packing facilities.

To carry out these duties, the office of hisbah would obviously require a staff of specialists trained in Islamic law as well as in land and wildlife management, engineering, agriculture and pathology. It would take time and effort to train these specialists and to set up educational programmes. Nevertheless for Shari'ah, Islamic law, to be fully carried out, the role of inspector and enforcer of standards lies with the muhtasib and qadi.

CONCLUSION

Islamic law contains its own special references that cover every aspect of desert reclamation. It sets its own values and aims as well as the principles that should govern the use of land, water, vegetation, livestock and wildlife. The institutions listed above are some of the ways through which desert reclamation can be carried out and all are well established in Islamic law. It is unfortunate that Muslim societies have forgotten these aims, principles and institutions.

Note

This chapter has been adapted from the author's extended paper, 'Desert reclamation and Islamic law', *The Muslim Scientist*, vol. 11, 1982, pp. 9–29, which also contains detailed bibliographical references.

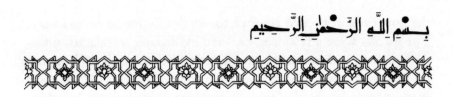

بِسْمِ اللَّهِ الرَّحْمَنِ الرَّحِيمِ

7 | THE DISCONNECTED PEOPLE

Fazlun M. Khalid

A TALE OF TWO PLACES

The rain was heavy and incessant, as rains usually are in Sarawak on the island of Borneo. The river was swollen but not unusually so. Ali, the Dyak tribesman, watched in dismay as his small patch of cultivated land crumbled into the river and was washed downstream.[1] He had to cross this same river to get to the logging company hut. His people practised shifting agriculture and his needs were immediate. But later, Ali will reflect on the fact that the river has swallowed not only his living but the ancient lifestyle of his people in one monsoon. His people lived in the forest of Sarawak for generations. They took from it what they needed and produced very little waste. What waste they produced went back into the soil, soon to become part of it as it decayed. The air was clean and it was quiet in this part of the forest except for the natural sounds of the people and animals, the wind, the rain and the river.

Now, all of that has changed since the arrival of the chain saws and tractors. There were profits to be made from the forest and the government needed revenue for its development programme. The forests were a resource, coveted by distant, voracious industrial countries, that could be used in the construction of shopping centres, recreation centres and other amenities. In order to meet these demands the logging companies continue to be given licences to fell the trees and export the logs, resulting in the clearance of massive tracts of land. As a consequence, the top soil is washed away into the river, the rivers silt up and the fish die. The animals that Ali and his community used to hunt are not to be found either since they have sought sanctuary deeper in the forest.

Ali does not know where to turn for help. His ancestral lands, his patch of cultivation and his home have all disappeared. His family and his community have scattered. He did not invite these strangers here and they did not bother to ask him if they could come. Someone from the government had come to his village to inform him that this was for the development and progress of his nation. But no one had ever come to speak to him about the good of the nation before, so why was it so necessary now? Decisions that affected his future were being taken in distant 'advanced countries' and their desire to improve their lifestyle resulted in the destruction of his. One day soon the land on which the forest stood will be covered with endless hectares of cash crops such as cocoa, coffee, palm oil, bananas, pineapple for consumers in the 'advanced countries'. Ali and his people will use very little or nothing of this themselves. They will be invaded by giant multinational companies and may be given no choice but to work for them in return for low wages and long hours. They will probably be told that what has happened will improve their standard of living. They will be bombarded by advertisements for things they never knew existed and had so far managed very well without. They will become consumers of very interesting and useless things made in faraway places and many will run up large debts in order to buy these things. They will become producers and consumers in the mega-markets of the world in less than a lifetime.

As yet, Ali knows nothing of this as with difficulty he crosses the swollen river and scrambles over the opposite bank into the company camp. He stumbles over dead tree stumps and squelches his way ankle deep in mud to the manager's hut. He calls the manager to the door, points to the gaping hole in the river bank opposite and complains bitterly,

'You have destroyed our lives. You are responsible.'

The logging camp manager, a minor cog in a big machine, was a kindly man. He had seen and heard this before and was well used to dealing with the situation. He listened sympathetically and then gave Ali 1,000 Malaysian dollars (about £220). The money came from what the company call the 'suspense account' that was provided to deal with these cases. Ali, his way of life and the traditions of his people were bought in a brief moment for a pittance.

There were other things Ali did not know. The trees that protected him would be transported and processed many times and a great deal of money would be made by other people in the process. The largest amount of money will be made by the people living furthest away from where the trees grew. The trees will go to Japan and other Pacific Basin countries. They will go to the West, to places like Britain and the rest of Europe. In Japan, it is likely that his trees, now turned into panels, would be used just once as casing for concrete on building sites and then discarded. In Britain, it is likely that Ali's trees will be turned into beautiful kitchens to adorn the houses in one of its many cities. The chances of Japanese construction workers and British housewives sparing a thought for the plight of Ali and his people are as remote as their houses are from the patch of land that Ali once tilled and which is now no more than silt in the sea.

Maryam lives a few thousand miles to the west of Ali's country. She is a Tuareg and her home once moved to and fro across the sands of the Sahara and the Sahel.[2] Her particular community are now settled as farmers in northern Nigeria. They are contemptuous of their present way of life but were driven there by the disastrous drought of the early 1970s.

The Tuareg are a nomadic people. They were and still are like a bridge across the Sahara. They cover the expanse of west central Sahara and the Sahel. That is an area roughly covered by what is today southern Algeria, south-west Libya, Niger and northern Mali. A generation ago they were almost wholly nomadic stock breeders. They were also caravan traders with their routes crisscrossing the Sahara in many directions. They exchanged their livestock, African gold and ivory for food, salt and Arabian and European goods. When the Europeans, particularly the French, came to this area things rapidly began to change. Lines began to appear on the map where no lines were before, cutting across ancient lifestyles and relations. The Tuareg were subjected to the influences of political boundaries determined by faraway people and were no longer free to graze their stocks and trade as before. Other people wanted to settle them down when the majority of the Tuareg had no desire for this. Governments in the area wanted to include them in the national systems of the country; they wanted to educate them and bring them into an economy based on cash and tax.

As pastoral nomads the Tuareg have maintained a balance with their environment since ultimately they depend on it for sustenance. It is the combined effects of drought, increased desertification (which meant that the wells and other resources were overused), and governmental pressure that restrict the movement of the Tuareg. The extreme climatic conditions that the Tuareg are suffering is thought by many scientists to be linked to the burning of fossil fuels in industrialized countries. This has contributed to what has been termed the 'greenhouse' effect and caused the earth's temperature to rise by an average 0.5 degrees Centigrade in the past century. We are told that of all the energy consumed in the past 2,000 years, over half has been consumed in this century. Of this over 80 per cent has been consumed by countries in the Northern hemisphere. The effect of this has been to push rainfall towards the poles and allow drier weather to spread towards the equator.[3] These temperature changes may seem small but the earth and biosphere are in such fine balance that they can cause massive and irreversible changes to people's lifestyles. Nature makes a mockery of national boundaries. For example, it has been known for the wind to drop tons of Saharan topsoil on vast areas of Europe as red rain.

But this is not the end of the story for Maryam and her people. Multinational companies will persuade them to use this or that fertilizer, this or that pesticide, this or that tractor. They will inevitably become consumers in a world market just like Ali and his people on the opposite side of the earth. Before all this happens somebody should remember to tell Maryam and her people that, according to the United Nations Environment Programme, one-third of the world's farmland will be desert by the year 2000.[4] By developing methods of agriculture and irrigation that can be sustained without importing expensive technology, and by balanced use of natural resources, parts of the desert can be farmed and can support local communities, but a large proportion of the marginal land that the Tuareg are now farming is better suited to their traditional nomadic lifestyle. Many of the Tuareg find that they have been pulled out of the desert only to be pushed back into it.

GOING NOWHERE FAST

The differences between Ali's and Maryam's lives are obvious, but what are the similarities? Firstly, they each belonged to a traditional people who had evolved a lifestyle unique to the environment in which they lived. Secondly, they lived in balance with their environment and thirdly, within the space of a generation or two, their lifestyles underwent sudden and drastic disruption. Now they lack control over their lives and are part of political structures and institutions which are not of their choosing. They have been deprived of their independent self-sustaining lifestyle and are forced into a global cash economy. They are now subject to the changes of commodity markets and interest rates which have more to do with the ups and downs of powerful industrial countries and nothing at all to do with their lives. Finally, they are Muslims, living in Muslim countries, although it must be said that traditional people living the world over have experienced similar tragic disruption to their lives.

In terms of the vast time scales of our Creator what happened to Ali and Maryam was sudden and violent. The life span of our planet is estimated at about 4.5 billion years and the human species has been on this earth for about 1/10,000th of the earth's life span. The major civilizations emerged in the latest 1 per cent of human existence. The age of atomic power and high technology only came about in the last half of the twentieth century at about 1/1,000,000,000th of the earth's life span. Our lives and our times may seem important to us and they obviously are, but compared to cosmic time our lives are very small fractions of seconds. Another matter that clouds our vision about the suddenness of these changes is the fact that our recent forebears have themselves lived through a period of change and upheaval. Permanence and familiarity have been traded for change and insecurity. We are born into a society that has already changed and we continue to live in it experiencing change all the time. Change is now a way of life for us and only recently have we begun to acknowledge that this is leading us to environmental catastrophe and social collapse. The Qur'an says this about time:

> By (the token of) time through the ages
> Verily man is in loss
> Except such as have faith, and do righteous deeds, and (join together) in the mutual teaching of truth, and of patience and constancy.

> (Qur'an 103:1–3)

Ali and Maryam have been defrauded of their very different but equally valid ways, which took centuries to evolve, in less than one lifetime. Their loss is a consequence of other people's greed and their futures are uncertain.

What we notice about all this, is that after centuries of gradual movement, the process we call history has suddenly accelerated.[5] To an independent observer in geo-stationary orbit over the mid-Atlantic for the past 500 years, which as we have seen is a comparatively short time, our actions might have looked frantic. As for the last 100 years this same observer will most probably conclude that our conduct verges on madness. Many analysts from widely differing backgrounds have come to the conclusion that history is accelerating and continues to do so at an ever increasing rate. What does this mean? We have seen how fuel consumption has accelerated. This kind of very rapid increase is described as exponential growth and in the context of this discussion it would not be far-fetched to call it explosive or frightening growth. There are enough examples around us to sustain this point which is that all areas of production, consumption, progress and development have grown exponentially in the past 500 years and are continuing to do so.

So the questions remain. Do we know that we are accelerating ourselves into oblivion? Do we know in what direction we as a species are moving?

THE NATURAL STATE

The earth is Allah's creation, a very small part of the rest of His creation which is an infinitely vast universe. We are at a stage in history when we have enough information at our disposal to lead us uniquely to the conclusion that everything is connected. We are part of a vast galaxy of stars that makes our solar system look tiny. Yet the sun that gives us life is 93 million miles away. The earth's companion, the moon, is a quarter of a million miles away, yet it controls our tides and has an influence over our weather systems. The protective atmospheric shell around the earth which is held to it by gravity, is proportionately no thicker than the skin of a potato. We are in fact being carried along in a sea of space, in a very finely engineered, self-regulating, space ship. Not very long ago, people who knew nothing at all about these things lived with an intuitive knowledge that recognized the earth for what it was and protected it in the way they went about their business. We now claim to be infinitely superior in knowledge to the ancients, but the savagery with which we treat the environment exceeds all bounds. We claim to belong to the high point of civilization. Yet, we are in the middle of a process that will destroy our life-support systems and consequently existence as we know it.

We say the earth has shrunk, it is getting to be an ever smaller place. By this we mean we know more about distant people and places and can get to them more quickly. Fifty years ago it would have taken us six to eight weeks to get to Ali's river. Today we can do this in a day or two. Ali is now a neighbour and we cannot go on uprooting his trees forever. We know Ali does not like it because it affects him immediately and directly. But we now know that Ali's trees must stay where they are, because if they do not it will affect us too. If the effect is not immediate it will sooner or later be direct. Similarly, our lifestyle with its excessive use of fossil fuels did not affect Maryam and her people immediately but, when it did, the effect was direct and as we have seen drastic. We have lost the art of living in the *fitra* state, that is the natural state, in balance and in harmony with creation. Recognizing that our every action affects other people, other species and other places both near and far, the Qur'an says:

> (God) most gracious
> It is He who has taught the Qur'an
> He has created man
> He has taught him speech (and intelligence)
> The sun and the moon follow courses (exactly) computed
> and the herbs and the trees both (alike) bow in adoration
> and the firmament has He raised high, and He has set up the balance (of justice)
> In order that ye may not transgress (due) balance
> So establish weight with justice and fall not short in the balance
> It is He who has spread out the earth for (his) creatures
> Therein is fruit and date palms, producing spathes (enclosing dates)
> Also corn with (its) leaves, and stalk for fodder and sweet smelling plants
> Then which of the favours of our Lord will ye deny?
>
> (Qur'an 55:1–13)

Everything is connected with each other and each with the whole. Evaporation from the sea rises as moist clouds, falls as rain, flows as rivers and returns to the sea again. Many things happen during this cycle. The seeds and roots wait for the rain in the soil surrounded by natural nutrients. The sun combines with the rain to produce food for people, fodder for animals, wood for fuel and for building shelters and useful artefacts, waste for turning into organic matter that returns to the soil as nutrients to await the next cycle. The water having done its work on the surface flows down into the water table and replenishes it until the rains return again. The rest flows into rivers providing sustenance for other communities further downstream. Stocks of fish are replenished providing protein for people. This was how it was not very long ago. But now? Rain contaminated with industrial smog falls as acid rain and destroys forests and corrodes mountains and buildings. Rivers are no longer clean and many thousands of miles of water are poisoned, contaminated by industrial and agricultural waste products. The fish have lost their habitat, the people their protein. Some rivers are dammed and others diverted, as part of national development programmes supported by the World Bank and the International Monetary Fund, disrupting lives and flooding villages, obliterating cultures in the name of progress. Local and international disputes occur over the control and distribution of water. The seas around the estuaries of rivers flowing through industrial countries receive increasing doses of heavy metal poison. The fish are contaminated. Disease is introduced into the food chain. The Qur'an says:

> See ye the seed that ye sow in the ground?
> Is it ye that cause it to grow or are We the cause?
> Were it our will, We could crumble it to dry powder and ye would be left in wonderment
> (Saying) 'We are indeed left with debts for (nothing)
> Indeed we are shut out (of the fruits of our labour)'
> See ye that the water which ye drink?
> Do ye bring it down (in rain) from the cloud or do We?
> Were it our will We could make it salt (and unpalatable) then why do ye not give thanks?
>
> (Qur'an 56:63–70)

The human species is connected to Allah's creation too, because we are part of it. This needs to be repeated because we have been behaving as a species apart, arrogant and selfish, taking diabolical liberties with the rest of creation. We are rampaging through the delicate balance of nature. Savaging other species to extinction. Robbing future generations of their inheritance. We have become so trapped in our self-indulgence we are not even aware of it.

Two basic kinds of decisions confront us in life. One is about how we relate to other people and the other about how we relate to the environment. However, most of our relations with other people sooner or later affect the environment. Purely person-to-person transactions are very small in number. The baby cries for attention and finds comfort in the mother's embrace. But when the baby cries for food and the mother feeds it, the nature of that transaction is different from the first, because on this occasion they both draw from the environment where the food originates. We

107

can safely conclude from this that very nearly all our decisions have something to do with the environment—taking from it, putting things back into it, shaping it, changing it, modifying it. The process of making decisions presents us with a range of choices and in order to be able to exercise choice Allah has given us the gift of free will and the ability to reason. This is unique to the human species. With this comes the twin concepts of guardianship and responsibility which place mankind, the supreme exploiter of resources, in a central and sensitive position. The Qur'an says, on guardianship:

> It is He (Allah) who has made you his viceregent on earth.
>
> (Qur'an 6:165)

On responsibility:

> ... for us is the (responsibility for) our deeds, and for you for your deeds ...
>
> (Qur'an 42:15)

The mandate from the Creator enables us to take from His creation enough to satisfy need and thus continue to maintain the fine balance He has established. That is to be aware of the limits. But those of us who are living in the richer countries have now grossly exceeded our limits. We have created a large number of wants that are without limits. The borderline between needs and wants can be recognized. The borderline between wants and greed is always unclear. Whilst needs can be defined wants cannot. This is why the idea of 'standards of living' means different things to different people. Ali and Maryam are hostages to our standards of living.

There is another range of decisions we make which moves beyond the person-to-person. They are the decisions we make collectively as a group, a community, a country. These decisions are political by nature and it will be difficult, if not impossible, to find political decisions that sooner or later do not involve the environment. This is why Islam does not make a distinction between politics and religion. Life is one whole. Our attitudes and behaviour in one area affect other areas. Everything is connected, which inevitably means that all economic activity is connected with the environment. This is why, in order for the environment to function in balance as it should, we should not cheat it and plunder it under the guise of improving our living standards. But, the economic institutions we have set up and function under do precisely that. The banks, the practice of charging interest, the stock markets, the commodity markets, are all part of a massive fraud and we are defrauding nobody but ourselves. (This is explained in the chapter on 'Trade and commerce in Islam'; the other chapters are also connected to this one and to each other in the same way.)

There is one inevitable conclusion to all this: each one of us is responsible for what is happening to our environment today. The effect of what we do is not confined to our own homes, neighbourhoods and countries. It is far-reaching and tragic as we have seen in the cases of Ali and Maryam. If the communities of these people still seem far away and remote then there is one disturbing and worrying event that connects us with them directly and that is the hole we have managed to make in the ozone layer above us. The shield that protects all of us is now weakening through the effects of our actions and the radiation that seeps through the cracks does not discriminate between people living in Asia, Africa, America and Europe.

Whilst being individuals and individualistic is important, how we have come to interpret this must change. Self-indulgence or selfishness is clumsily hidden in the idea of improving oneself. It is connected with the idea of 'the quality of life' which, like 'standards of living', is misleading. This has led us to compete with each other as consumers, as individuals and as countries sucking things out of the earth at an ever-increasing rate and discharging a level of waste which the earth cannot recycle, thus contributing to the rapid destruction of the habitats and lifestyles of the weakest amongst us.

There are now a few things we can say in summary about ourselves that may give us an understanding of how we have reached a situation where we have put our home, the earth, under severe strain. As we have just seen, our attitude as individuals has not helped. We are invited to compete feverishly with each other to get the most out of the finite resources on earth. This means that we constantly exceed our limits. We all want more, to be and

109

look better, to be bigger, to be faster, to be grander, to be richer. We have also lost the ability to distinguish between need and greed, or we are simply not interested in the difference. We have lost the intuitive knowledge of relating to each other, to nature and to the environment. And as a result of this we have lost a sense of proportion and balance. All these are symptoms of a disconnected people. We have an image about what we need and what we want and we obscure the truth about ourselves. We are people on the wrong side of the great divide who cannot distinguish between stability and familiarity on the one hand and perpetual change and alienation on the other. We have discarded the fitra way of living for a lifestyle that is illusory and artificial. To relearn how all things in Allah's creation are interrelated and to realize that we are part of the same, we could do no better than to go to people like Ali and Maryam and absorb what they have to give before it is too late. The Qur'an says:

> Do no mischief on the
> Earth after it has been
> set in order. . .

(Qur'an 7:85)

The role model for us is the Prophet of Islam (S). The model of generosity, compassion and moderation. When he was asked by a companion about the most virtuous act of giving he said:

> Give away what you have while you are in good health, and while you have a keen desire to amass wealth, and while you are afraid of adversity and while you are longing for money. Do not wait to give your wealth away until you are dying . . .

(*Riyadh as Salihin*)

For us the first step towards this is to think about the way we take and the effect this has on other people, other species and other places.

References

1 For further information on the Dyak see *The Atlas of Man*, Marshall Cavendish, London, 1981.
2 Ibid., for further information on the Tuareg.
3 *The Gaia Atlas of Planet Management*, Pan Books, London, 1985.
4 André Singer, *Battle for the Planet*, Channel Four Books, 1987.
5 Gerard Piel, 'The acceleration of history' in Ritchie Calder (ed.), *The Future of a Troubled World*, Heinemann, London, 1983.